Symptoms and Solutions

DOG CARE
Companions

Symptoms and Solutions

The Ultimate Home Health Guide— What to Watch for, What to Do

From the Editors of

Pets
part of the family

Edited by Matthew Hoffman

Consultant: Lowell Ackerman, D.V.M., Ph.D., Diplomate A.C.V.D., a veterinary dermatologist in private practice in Mesa, Arizona, and author of *Skin and Haircoat Problems in Dogs* and *Owner's Guide to Dog Health*

RODALE

Pets: Part of the Family public television series
is generously underwritten by PETsMART,
PETsMART.com, and Fresh Step cat litter.

Notice

This book is intended as a reference volume only, not as a medical manual. The information given here is designed to help you make informed decisions about your pet's health. It is not intended as a substitute for any treatment that may have been recommended by your veterinarian. If you suspect that your pet has a serious medical problem, we urge you to seek competent help.

Library of Congress Cataloging-in-Publication Data

Symptoms & solutions : the ultimate home health guide—what to watch for, what to do /

from the editors of Pets, part of the family : edited by Matthew Hoffman ;

consultant, Lowell Ackerman.

      p.   cm. — (Dog care companions)

Includes index.

ISBN 1–57954–114–3 hardcover

1. Dogs—Diseases. 2. Handbooks, manuals, etc. I. Hoffman, Matthew. II. Pets, part of the family.

III. Title: Symptoms and solutions. IV. Series.

SF991.S97 1999

636.7'089—dc21   99–15693

ISBN 1–57954–259–X paperback

Distributed to the book trade by St. Martin's Press

2 4 6 8 10 9 7 5 3 1 hardcover
2 4 6 8 10 9 7 5 3 1 paperback

OUR PURPOSE

To explore, celebrate, and stand in awe
before the special relationship between us
and the animals who share our lives.

Symptoms and Solutions

CONTRIBUTING WRITERS
Lowell Ackerman, Susan McCullough, Brad Swift, Kim Thornton,
Elaine Waldorf Gewirtz, Christine Wilford

RODALE ACTIVE LIVING BOOKS
Editor: Matthew Hoffman
Publisher: Neil Wertheimer
Editorial Director: Michael Ward
Research Manager: Ann Gossy Yermish
Copy Manager: Lisa D. Andruscavage
Cover Designer and Design Coordinator: Joanna Reinhart
Associate Studio Manager: Thomas P. Aczel
Book Manufacturing Director: Helen Clogston
Manufacturing Manager: Mark Krahforst

WELDON OWEN PTY LTD
Chief Executive Officer: John Owen
President: Terry Newell
Publisher: Sheena Coupe
Associate Publisher: Lynn Humphries
Senior Editor: Janet Healey
Project Editor: Janine Flew
Senior Designer: Kylie Mulquin
Designer: Robyn Latimer
Illustrators: Virginia Gray, Chris Wilson/Merilake
Icons: Matt Graif, Chris Wilson/Merilake
Indexer: Garry Cousins
Production Manager: Caroline Webber
Production Assistant: Kylie Lawson

Film separation by Colourscan Co. Pte. Ltd., Singapore

CONTENTS

Introduction

Unless you're lucky enough to have a veterinarian in the family, any change in your dog's usual behavior is sure to raise a lot of questions. Is it serious? Is she hurting? Do I need to call the vet?

No one wants to ignore something that might be serious. On the other hand, why head for the emergency room for something that's really a minor problem?

I've made both mistakes. One night about a year ago, I woke up at midnight because Molly, my Labrador, was retching in a corner of the bedroom. I turned on the light and saw an awful-looking mess on the carpet. She was heaving so hard I was afraid she'd hurt herself. I rushed her to an emergency veterinarian across town. "Dogs throw up all the time," he said after giving Molly a brief examination. "It was just something she ate."

Sure enough, by the time we walked out the door, Molly was in great spirits and having the time of her life—and I was more than a little embarrassed about having acted like an overprotective parent.

I remembered that night several months later when I noticed that Molly was straining to pee. She didn't seem especially uncomfortable, and I figured she'd be fine. All day she kept asking to go outside, but once outdoors, she still couldn't go. I finally got worried enough to call our vet—who told me to bring her in immediately. Molly, it turned out, had a bladder stone. She might not have made it if I'd waited much longer. That one was close—and scary.

Dog-lovers run into this dilemma all the time. Dogs can't say what's wrong or where it hurts. It's up to us to notice their symptoms and decide whether or not they need professional care. Sometimes the decision is easy. You're not likely to worry a lot when your dog has a cut paw pad or a bit of diarrhea. But what if there's blood in the diarrhea? What if her nose has changed color or she has a fever or she hasn't eaten all day? Until now, there's never been a book that tells exactly how to recognize common symptoms and take the right action.

Symptoms and Solutions may be the most important pet-care book you'll ever own because it discusses more than 50 of the most common symptoms dogs get, from appetite loss and blood in the urine to stool changes and weight loss. You'll learn which symptoms can be handled at home and which need emergency first-aid or a veterinarian's advice. And you'll learn how to help your dog get better.

Suppose your dog is suddenly squinting. Nine times out of 10 it means she has grit in the eye and you can flush the eye with saline to wash out the grit. But squinting can also be a symptom of glaucoma, which may cause blindness when it's not treated quickly. *Symptoms and Solutions* will help you know the difference. (Here's a great tip: When only one eye is affected, you can be pretty sure it's caused by irritation. When something's wrong with both eyes, call your vet because it's probably something more serious.)

This is much more than just a guide to symptoms. It's packed with effective, practical treatments—things you can do at home to help your dog feel better and also to treat the underlying problem. A simple "water cure" that may clear up blood in the urine. Over-the-counter antihistamines that stop allergy symptoms. The best ways to get rid of worms. A nutritional cure for a dry coat. And hundreds more.

To make this book completely practical and easy-to-use, we've included more than 140 color photographs and illustrations, along with great tips from the country's top veterinarians. You'll learn to be alert to changes you probably never noticed before—the hundreds of little signs and signals that will let you know when your dog isn't feeling well and needs some help.

Best of all, *Symptoms and Solutions* gives the gift of confidence. You'll know that when your dog does get sick or hurt, you'll spot the problem quickly and know what to do. And when you're caring for your dog, nothing is better than that.

Matthew Hoffman

Matthew Hoffman
Editor, *Pets: Part of the Family* books

PART ONE

IN SICKNESS AND IN HEALTH

No one knows your dog's habits, moods, likes,
and dislikes better than you. You'll notice changes in daily
routines as soon as they occur—changes that could
give valuable clues as to what's going on.

CHAPTER ONE

How to Read Symptoms

Dogs don't wear neon signs that tell you when they're sick, and it's never easy to tell whether their symptoms are serious or not. When you know a few things to look for, however, you can make some pretty good guesses about what's going on.

Most dogs go to the vet once or twice a year for shots and a checkup. Annual exams are essential, but there are limits to what veterinarians can learn during a 30-minute visit. If a dog was a little achy before, but is fine on the day of the exam, his vet won't suspect that he's having hip problems or the beginnings of arthritis. And the people in the family won't know either, unless they have been keeping tabs on his health. This is why knowing how to read symptoms is so important: It allows you to discover problems before they have a chance to get serious.

There are many complicated definitions of a symptom, but basically it's any change that you can notice, says Joanne Howl, D.V.M., a veterinarian in private practice in West River, Maryland. Symptoms can be physical, such as a runny nose or a limp, or they can involve behavior, such as restlessless. Not all changes that occur in a dog's life are symptoms, of course. There has to be something abnormal about the change, says Dr. Howl. A dog who starts panting when the weather turns hot obviously doesn't have a symptom. On the other hand, panting that occurs for no obvious reason may indeed be a symptom. "A symptom is the disease leaving you a little clue," says Dr. Howl.

Types of Symptoms

Apart from taking your dog to the vet for regular exams, about the best thing you can do for his health is learn how to read symptoms, says Robin Downing, D.V.M., a veterinarian in private practice in Windsor, Colorado. This doesn't mean that you have to know every possible symptom, chapter and verse. It does mean learning to make educated guesses. Is a symptom likely to be serious or not? Will it go away or will it get worse? Should you call your vet right away, or can it wait until tomorrow?

Individual symptoms can be hard to interpret, but by learning a few general principles, you'll get a very good idea of how seriously to take various symptoms and whether you need to act quickly, in the near future, or, if you're lucky, not at all.

Is it normal? One reason symptoms are so hard to interpret is that they're essentially moving targets. "What's a symptom in one dog may not be a symptom in another," says Dr. Howl. "Suppose your dog has a runny nose. You have to ask yourself whether that's normal for him. Some dogs have runny noses and some don't. If he doesn't usually have a runny nose, then it's a symptom."

What else is happening? By about the third day of medical school, vets have learned that a single symptom, viewed in isolation from other physical or emotional things that may be happening, is just about meaningless. That's why vets don't conclude an exam as soon as you describe a symptom; that's when the questions really start. Suppose your dog has a slight fever. If nothing else is happening—he hasn't had diarrhea, his energy is good, he's eating well, and his coat looks healthy—your vet may conclude that the fever is probably just a natural and temporary rise in his usual temperature and isn't anything to worry about. On the other hand, a fever that's accompanied by another symptom or symptoms becomes a little more meaningful.

Is it local or general? This is a very important question because it can help you understand just how sick your dog is. It's not an absolute rule, but symptoms that occur locally—that is, only in one place—tend to be less serious than those that occur generally, says Dr. Howl. A dog with a hard-to-heal sore on his nose, for example, may just be suffering the consequences of using his nose as a shovel. A dog with multiple sores, and perhaps other symptoms such as fever, has more of a widespread problem.

It's certainly possible, of course, for local symptoms to be serious. Cancer caused by sun exposure, for example, can cause a single sore. So you can't assume that local symptoms are inconsequential. But knowing which symptoms are local and which are general will help you form a clearer overall picture of your dog's health.

Is it acute or chronic? Symptoms that come on suddenly are called acute symptoms, while chronic symptoms may have been months or years in the making. Symptoms often appear in different ways depending on whether they're acute or chronic. "The ones that are dramatic and come on quite suddenly usually need rapid attention—and often go away just as quickly," says Dr. Howl. "The ones that come on slowly may be more difficult to cure."

A good example of an acute symptom is a cut on the paw. It occurred suddenly, and even if the cut is deep, it won't be difficult to treat. Arthritis, however, is a chronic condition that starts out small and gradually gets worse. It's harder to

Your veterinarian only sees your dog once or twice a year, while you see things every day. You should trust your instincts and tell your vet everything that has you worried.

treat than acute problems, for two reasons: Not only is there the initial damage to the joint but also years of arthritis will have stimulated the body to fight back—and that battle makes the original problem even worse, Dr. Howl explains.

Is it intermittent or constant? You can make some good guesses about the causes of symptoms by noticing whether they come and go or stick around. "If your dog is limping, and he keeps limping for a week, it's probably an injury," says Dr. Howl. "If the limping comes and goes, it's more likely to be bodywide, maybe caused by arthritis or Lyme disease."

Rating Symptoms

Veterinarians have long lists of symptoms that are almost always serious, such as bleeding that doesn't stop, extremely high fevers, or abdominal swelling. Most dogs will never have one of these extreme—and obvious—symptoms. Instead, they'll have a symptom or a combination of symptoms that you just can't make up your mind about. Do you rush out the door to see your vet or wait around to see what happens? You may not even be sure whether what you're seeing is a symptom or just a normal, if unusual, change. "The biggest giveaway is when your dog just feels bad," says Dr. Howl. "A dog can't tell you what's going on, but he won't lie to you either. When he's moping around, he's probably feeling really sick, and that's a perfectly good reason to call your vet."

Of course, some dogs are more stoic than others. A big, tough Rottweiler might limp dramatically if he bruises his paw, while a diminutive poodle may act as though everything's normal even when she's burning up with fever.

It's not scientific, but Dr. Howl has her own technique for reading beneath the surface. "The best way to get a feel for what's going on is to put yourself in your pet's place," she says. "If there's a sore on his nose, and you'd be scared if that sore were on you, then you need to get help. Even though dogs are different from people, their bodies respond in very similar ways."

EMOTIONAL CHANGES, PHYSICAL SIGNS

We usually think of symptoms as being physical, like a cut or a fever. But symptoms can also involve behavior, such as sudden aggressiveness, a change in sleeping habits, or profound fatigue. Many changes in behavior mean that dogs are worried, anxious, or stressed, but they can also be signs of physical problems. A dog who's lethargic, not eating, and generally moping about could have pancreatitis, thyroid disease, or even heartworms.

Even if the underlying problem turns out to be a behavioral or emotional one, the symptoms, such as not eating, can make a dog physically ill. That's why veterinarians recommend taking dogs for a checkup if their moods don't return to normal within a few days.

CHAPTER TWO

WHEN TO CALL YOUR VET

No one wants to ignore a symptom that might be serious, but no one
wants to rush to the vet every week, either. Knowing a few common symptoms
will help you decide what's serious and what's not.

If people took their dogs to the veterinarian every time they got sick, or every time they thought they were sick, they'd get the automotive equivalent of frequent flier miles. Dogs are always doing something—throwing up, having diarrhea, or walking away from their food with glazed looks in their eyes—that makes even calm people a little bit nervous.

But apart from the occasional cold or digestive complaint, dogs are remarkably hardy animals who often go their entire lives without a serious illness. It doesn't hurt that their owners are always alert to changes and are prepared to take care of small problems before they turn into something worse.

That's really the key to keeping dogs healthy—recognizing potential problems early. But it's not always easy to do. Even veterinarians are often puzzled as to whether a symptom is truly serious or just a passing thing, says Craig N. Carter, D.V.M., Ph.D., head of epidemiology at the Texas Veterinary Medical Diagnostic Laboratory at Texas A&M University in College Station.

Trusting Your Instincts

In a way, dog owners have an advantage over veterinarians: They live with their dogs every

People who live, play, and hang out with their dogs can tell very quickly when they're feeling good and when they're under the weather.

day and can tell in an instant when they're feeling or acting differently than usual. Veterinarians are trained observers, but they only see their patients once or twice a year, says Dr. Carter. It's tricky for them to know whether the way a dog is acting is normal for him or whether there's something wrong.

"I depend on owners and their interpretations," says Ken Drobatz, D.V.M., associate professor of critical care at the Veterinary Hospital of the University of Pennsylvania in Philadelphia. "People know their dogs a lot better than their veterinarians do."

There are limits to instincts, of course. If your dog's symptoms resemble something you've seen before, you'll be more confident about deciding whether to call your vet. But some symptoms you'll see will be unfamiliar or simply too serious to take chances with. You need to call for help any time you're on unfamiliar ground, says Dr. Carter.

Nine Symptoms to Worry About

Veterinarians have identified thousands of symptoms and combinations of symptoms caused by various conditions. You don't need to know them all, of course—that's what your vet is for. But you should know the main symptoms that always mean you need some help.

Breathing problems. This is one of the easiest symptoms to recognize, and also the most dangerous. Dogs who pant heavily when they're resting or are struggling to breathe could have heart or lung problems, says Elizabeth Rozanski, D.V.M., a specialist in emergency and critical care at Tufts University Veterinary Medical Center in North Grafton, Massachusetts.

Even if the underlying cause of the symptom isn't serious, difficulty breathing may reduce the flow of oxygen to the heart and other organs, possibly causing permanent damage. It's essential to get help quickly, Dr. Rozanski says.

Pale gums. As with breathing problems, pale gums are a sign that tissues in the body aren't getting enough blood and oxygen. Except in dogs whose gums are naturally dark, the gums should be bright pink. Many conditions, including internal bleeding and heart disease, can cause the gums to turn pale. Pale gums are nearly always an emergency, says Dr. Rozanski.

Unusual fatigue. Dogs have energy ups and downs just as people do, and there will always be days when they try to turn back on walks or don't want to get out of bed in the morning. Fatigue that lasts more than a day, however, or that seems unusually severe, warrants calling your vet. "Many of the dogs I can think of with major problems initially had lethargy that did not get better within a day or two," says Dr. Rozanski.

Swollen abdomen. You don't have to worry too much about this if you have a small dog, but the big, deep-chested breeds, such as Great Danes and Doberman pinschers, have a high risk of bloat, a condition in which the stomach suddenly fills with gas and expands.

Bloat is always an emergency, and it can develop within hours. It's essential to recognize the warning signs: abdominal swelling, restless behavior, and heavy, labored breathing, says Dr. Rozanski.

Sudden injuries. Dogs are flexible, strong, and covered by protective fur, which means that they can be involved in serious accidents, such as getting hit by a car, without showing a mark. But appearances can be deceiving. Anything that hits a dog hard enough to knock him down has the potential to cause internal injuries that may not produce symptoms until hours or days later. No matter how good your dog looks after an accident, take him in for a checkup, Dr. Rozanski advises.

STRANGE SYMPTOMS

We often assume that Nature designed the body with all due care and consideration, and that physical symptoms are always helpful warning signs. This is usually the case, but dogs do a few things that can only be described as strange. For example:

• **The reverse sneeze.** Dogs will periodically make a noise that sounds something like "whoosie," in which air rushes into the nose with a wheezing sound. Veterinarians call it a reverse sneeze, and it doesn't mean much of anything—although it may be caused by intermittent allergies.

• **Eating dung.** Nearly all dogs have sampled dung, either their own or that from other pets. Apart from increasing their risk of getting parasites, it's not a serious problem.

• **Sexual knot.** After mating, the female's muscles contract and the male's penis swells. The resulting "tie" will often keep them together for 30 minutes or more—presumably to increase the odds of conception. It's a strange sight, but it's normal, and most dogs will unlock on their own. If they don't, putting an ice pack on the male's testicles may help.

Chemical breath. Dogs will put their noses into just about anything, including the chemicals that people keep in the garage or under the sink. Even when the stuff they eat isn't marked "poison," it may still be toxic. You could have only an hour—or less—to start treatment.

Unless you actually saw your dog lapping a puddle or pulling his nose from a bag, poisoning can be hard to recognize. Pay attention if you see a tipped-over bottle or a bag that's been torn open. Some dogs will have a chemical smell to their breath, or they'll be dizzy or vomiting.

Severe digestive problems. Because of their adventuresome appetites, some dogs have digestive upsets fairly regularly. Occasional vomiting and diarrhea aren't problems for most adult dogs. In puppies, however, they can be serious. "Puppies don't have very good reserves and can get dehydrated or develop low blood sugar quickly," Dr. Rozanski explains. "Excessive vomiting would be more than once an hour or more than six times in an eight-hour period," she adds.

Straining to urinate. If anything, most dogs urinate too much, or at least too often, especially when you're trying to walk somewhere in a hurry. A dog who is straining to urinate, however, could have kidney problems or a blockage in the urinary tract. Accumulations of urine can put a great deal of pressure on the bladder, in some cases causing it to rupture, says Dr. Rozanski.

Changes in the eyes. Most eye changes, such as redness or excessive tears, are fairly minor and will clear up quickly, either on their own or with the help of antibiotics. But the same symptoms that indicate minor eye problems can also be caused by glaucoma, which may cause blindness if it's not treated quickly. Any change in the appearance of the eyes needs to be checked out by a vet, says Dr. Rozanski.

Watchful Waiting

Veterinarians are naturally cautious. While some symptoms always need quick treatment, many others don't—at least not right away. A dog who throws up once, for example, is probably fine. A dog who keeps throwing up is going to need some help. As a compromise between rushing into treatment and ignoring a problem, veterinarians have a category of treatment called watchful waiting. It means watching a dog closely to make sure that he's actually getting better. Here are some of the symptoms that usually require watchful waiting.

Diarrhea. If your dog's bowels are working overtime, but he generally seems okay, it's fine to wait a day to see if he improves. Just be sure to keep his water bowl full since he'll need to drink in order to replace the fluids that the diarrhea is taking out, says Dr. Drobatz.

Vomiting. Dogs do it all the time. They get a viral infection or eat something nasty, and pitch up their suppers—and then go about their business. Dogs who keep vomiting over a period of hours or days, however, may have something more serious wrong and will need to be checked out.

Bloody urine. Most of the time blood in urine isn't a big deal. It usually means that a dog has a urinary tract infection, says James Wohl, D.V.M., assistant professor of emergency medicine at Auburn University School of Veterinary Medicine in Auburn, Alabama. Many

infections go away on their own within a few days, but you'll still want to see your vet to make sure the infection doesn't get worse, he advises.

Skipping meals. It's natural for the appetite to wax and wane. Dogs usually eat less in summer and more in winter, and temporary illnesses such as flu can put a dent in their appetites. Dogs can safely go a day or two without food. If your dog continues to skip meals or has other symptoms such as fever, you'll want to call your vet, says Dr. Wohl.

Persistent scratching. Most of the things that cause itching, such as allergies and fleas, are fairly easy to treat at home—either by getting rid of the underlying cause of the itching or by treating the symptom itself. The problem with persistent scratching is that dogs can damage the skin, causing hard-to-heal sores or infections. It's worth asking your veterinarian what the problem is and whether there's a long-term treatment that's likely to be effective.

Scratching is a symptom of several persistent conditions, including fleas and allergies.

CHAPTER THREE

THE PREVENTION PLAN

Many of the illnesses that dogs get can be prevented with simple home care.
When you know what to look for and what to do, you can help ensure
that your dog will have a longer, healthier, happier life.

Dogs took pretty good care of themselves before people came along, but their lives tended to be more stressful than those enjoyed by dogs today. The wild life is a lot tougher than domesticity. Our dogs don't risk their lives to get dinner, or eat spoiled carcasses to keep from starving. They don't have to break through snow and ice to get a drink of water, and they don't have to fight for territory and shelter. Not surprisingly, dogs today are living longer than they used to, says Agnes Rupley, D.V.M., a veterinarian in private practice in College Station, Texas.

But living in the lap of luxury brings some problems with it. Many veterinarians believe that modern commercial foods and contemporary lifestyles, such as a lack of exercise, have led to an increase in a variety of health threats, including allergies, diabetes, and arthritis.

It's not that dogs would be healthier if they went back to their wild ways. But they would do better if we all made an effort to combine the best parts of the old ways, which included regular exercise and lots of interaction with fellow dogs, with the best of the new, such as good hygiene and regular checkups. Preventive care isn't expensive (it's a heck of a lot cheaper than veterinary care), and it doesn't take a lot of time.

And the payoff is tremendous: a small amount of time for a lifetime of love.

Eating Well

Most dogs aren't very picky about food. They'll stuff themselves with just about anything, from their usual kibble to whatever they can filch from the counter. They aren't thinking about their weight or their teeth. They're just thinking about food—and when the next meal is going to be served. What they don't think about—but we

Dogs are happiest when they spend time with other dogs. A rich social life teaches them to be adventuresome and outgoing. It helps them learn proper canine manners as well.

9

do—is whether what goes in their bowls is good for them. Dogs who eat wholesome, nutritious foods are much less likely to be overweight. They're less likely to get diabetes and other digestive problems. A healthful diet may even reduce the risk of kidney stones.

Choosing the right food can be tricky. Most vets recommend avoiding generic, "no-name" foods. Even though they're often half the cost of name-brand foods, they're not made with top-quality ingredients. There's nothing wrong with going to the other extreme and buying high-cost premium foods, which are available from veterinarians and pet supply stores. Premium foods are made from excellent ingredients, and vets sometimes recommend them for dogs with special needs, such as unusually active dogs.

For most dogs, however, premium foods won't make a big difference in their health. Unless your vet has suggested otherwise, you can't go wrong buying the less expensive, name-brand foods at the supermarket.

The main problem with modern diets is that dogs tend to eat more than they need, and the extra weight can shave years from their lives. "Preventing excessive weight gain is not your dog's responsibility," says Rance Sellon, D.V.M., a veterinarian at Washington State University in Pullman. "Where that number lands on the scales is in your control."

Measure what goes in the bowl. Veterinarians have found that when people guess how much they feed their dogs and then actually measure the amounts, they're amazed how much they're really giving. Dr. Sellon recommends measuring the food all the time. Not only will you be able to control more precisely how much your dog eats, you'll also notice when he's eating more or less than usual, which can provide additional clues about his health.

Keep track of treats. When you're trying to figure out how much your dog is eating, don't forget to consider the little extras—the biscuits, beef strips, or tasty table scraps. Treats—both the commercial and homemade varieties—are generally high in fat and calories and can sabotage the best-planned diet. Veterinarians recommend cutting back on treats or replacing them with healthier snacks, such as pieces of fruit or vegetables cut in bite-size pieces. Many dogs like popcorn as well.

Cut calories a little at a time. Since dogs who are overweight have a higher risk for so many different conditions, veterinarians believe a weight-loss plan is essential. The easiest way to do it is to cut back the amount you feed your dog by 25 percent. Most dogs will start losing weight within a few weeks. If he doesn't start slimming down, cut the amount of food again by up to 25 percent. If he still doesn't lose weight, you'll need to talk to your vet about a different kind of plan.

Feed them at certain times. Some dogs show admirable restraint at the dinner table, but most will eat whatever goes in the bowl. If you keep it full all the time, they will eat all the time. Vets recommend putting pets on strict eating schedules—feeding them once in the morning and again in the evening, for example.

Satisfy the cravings. A well-planned diet may be great for a dog's health, but it isn't likely to win his heart. Dogs don't like diets any more than people do, and you will probably see an increase in begging, whining, and mooching.

KNOWING WHAT'S NORMAL

The reason dogs don't come with checklists of things to watch out for is that every dog is different, physically and emotionally. The only way to know when your dog is getting sick is to know what he's like when he's healthy. Vets refer to this as a dog's baseline. Any change from his baseline—meaning his habits, appearance, and moods—means something's going on that you need to watch, says Stan Coe, D.V.M., a veterinarian in private practice in Seattle.

• **Watch how much he eats.** One of the first signs of illness is a change in appetite. Veterinarians recommend measuring a dog's food every day. This makes it easy to know when he's eating more or less than usual. "It's also important to notice if your dog is more reluctant to chew hard kibble, which may signal a problem in his mouth," says Rance Sellon, D.V.M., a veterinarian at Washington State University in Pullman.

• **Watch how much he drinks.** It's normal for a dog's thirst to fluctuate with the seasons and the amount of exercise he's getting, but dramatic changes can indicate serious problems such as diabetes, kidney failure, or adrenal gland problems.

• **Watch his bathroom habits.** You don't have to get up close and personal, but taking a quick look at your dog's urine and stools can provide a lot of information in a hurry. Any change in their usual appearance may be a warning sign, says Dr. Coe.

• **Check his endurance and energy.** A dog who was always laid back and then is suddenly hyper-energized could have a hormonal problem. Similarly, when a dog who was always an energy powerhouse suddenly is tired all the time, you can be pretty sure that something's wrong.

• **Look at his eyes.** Dogs' eyes should always be clear and bright. A change in color or the appearance of more tears is worth watching.

• **Look in his mouth.** Take a look at the teeth and gums now and then. The gums should be pink and firm, and the teeth should be relatively clean. Gums that look red or irritated, or breath that almost knocks you over mean there's something wrong—either in the mouth itself or elsewhere in the body.

• **Feel his skin.** It's normal for dogs to get a bit lumpy as they get older, but lumps can also be a warning sign of cancer. As a rule, lumps that feel soft and roll freely beneath the skin are less likely to be a worry than those that are hard and fixed in place.

• **Get professional advice.** "Before a dog enters his later years, he should visit the vet once a year for a general health exam," says Dr. Sellon. Older dogs need to go in more often, usually two or three times a year.

THE CANINE MEDICINE CHEST

Veterinarians recommend that people put together a first-aid kit or medicine chest that's specifically for dogs. You can certainly do this, but most of the time it's not necessary because many medicines that people use work just as well for dogs. Here are the basics you'll want to keep on hand.

• Activated charcoal for treating poisoning; your veterinarian will tell you how much to give

• Aloe vera lotion, or the whole plant, for treating minor burns

• Betadine or another solution for cleaning wounds

• Buffered or coated aspirin for fever or miscellaneous aches and pains; give one-quarter of a 325-milligram tablet for every 10 pounds of weight, once or twice a day

• Colloidal oatmeal for relieving itching caused by fleas or allergies

• Epsom salts for cleaning and soaking wounds or sores

• Hydrogen peroxide (3 percent solution) to induce vomiting; give one tablespoon for every 15 to 20 pounds of weight

• Over-the-counter hydrocortisone cream for treating minor inflammation

• Pepto-Bismol for diarrhea and other digestive complaints; give one teaspoon for every 20 pounds of weight every four hours

• Saline solution for flushing grit from the eyes and soothing irritation

• Triple antibiotic ointment or cream

• Witch hazel for soothing minor inflammations as well as insect bites and stings

---

To help them feel more satisfied, add a tablespoon or two of canned pumpkin to their food, says Craig N. Carter, D.V.M., Ph.D., head of epidemiology at the Texas Veterinary Medical Diagnostic Laboratory at Texas A&M University in College Station. It's high in fiber, low in calories, and it's filling—and most dogs love the taste, too.

Put the trash away. Your dog's ancestors thrived on eating everything they could find, but modern dogs aren't accustomed to such varied menus, says Dr. Rupley. Food-foraging and trash-mongering aren't likely to do them too much damage in the long run, but they can upset their stomachs in a big way. And it's not unheard of for dogs to eat large objects such as bones, or even paper or plastic, which can clog up the digestive tract, Dr. Rupley adds.

Give them dry foods. Even though canned and semi-moist foods provide good nutrition and dogs love them, they're not very good for the teeth, says John Hamil, D.V.M., a veterinarian in private practice in Laguna Beach, California. Unlike dry kibble, moist foods don't help keep the teeth clean by scouring them with each bite. And because wet foods stick to the teeth, bacteria are more likely to multiply and cause infections and inflammation.

Store foods in their own containers.
Removing dry dog food from its bag to store it
for long periods in a plastic container can allow
the plastic flavor and chemicals to leach into the
dog's food. "Dog food is usually better off stored
inside its own bag, which can be put inside a
plastic container to maintain freshness without
risking contamination," Dr. Rupley says.

Staying Active

Keeping dogs busy with regular exercise is
among the most powerful strategies for keeping
them trim, healthy, and content. Exercise keeps
the heart and lungs working well. It strengthens
muscles and ligaments so that they are better
able to protect the joints. It even makes pets less
likely to misbehave. Many common behavior
problems, such as digging holes or chewing on
furniture, are caused by boredom, especially
when dogs don't have outlets for their energy.

"Some of the benefits of 'survival of the
fittest' were lost with domestication, especially
the exercise from chasing and being chased,"
adds Stan Coe, D.V.M., a veterinarian in private
practice in Seattle.

How much exercise do dogs need? It really
depends on the breed. Terriers and herding and
sporting dogs are energy dynamos. They typically need an hour or more of vigorous exercise
a day to stay happy and healthy. Dogs that are
extra-large or extra-small tend to be more laid
back and can get by with one or two fairly short
walks a day. Generally, all dogs need at least 30
minutes of exercise a day—15 minutes in the
morning and 15 more in the evening. If your
dog hasn't been getting much exercise lately,

*One of the most important preventive medicines is
plenty of exercise—and because dogs like it, they'll
never give it up.*

take it slowly at first. Take a couple of walks each
day, preferably along a route without too many
hills. Or play in the yard or the living room for
a few minutes at a time. As he starts getting in
better shape, you can increase the intensity—
and explore other, more exciting ways of getting
his paws moving.

One of the best fitness plans—and one that
dogs love—is cross-training, in which they do
a variety of activities such as swimming,
walking, running, or chasing a ball. Swimming
is particularly good for dogs who like the water
because it works all the muscles and is easy on
the joints. Of course, it's important to supervise
a dog in the water. This includes making sure
that he can get out of the water and avoiding
rivers and the ocean, where fast-moving cur-
rents can pose hidden dangers. And don't be
surprised if your dog refuses to get wet. Some
dogs simply don't like the water, and you can't
force them to have a good time.

There is one exercise caution: Avoid doing hard exercise involving twists and turns on asphalt or cement. These surfaces are too slippery for dogs' feet to get a grip on, and the slipping and sliding are hard on their feet and joints.

Basic Hygiene

Unless dogs are active on the show circuit or are otherwise on public display, they don't have to be bathed very often. Their skin is loaded with oil-producing glands that keep it supple and healthy. Every dog is different, however. The short-coated breeds usually don't need a lot of attention, says Dr. Coe. But dogs with long coats need regular bathing and brushing—not only to look and smell good, but to reduce the risk of skin infections.

Regular grooming provides another bonus as well. It's a great way to find problems that you might otherwise miss, such as fleas in the fur or small bumps on the skin.

Even though grooming needs vary widely according to the breed and your dog's particular habits, here's what vets usually recommend.

Brush them often. Regular brushing distributes natural oils over the skin, which can help prevent rashes and infections. Short-haired pets can be brushed or rubbed with a chamois or soft cloth once a week, while those with longer fur should really be brushed daily, if only for a few minutes.

Get rid of hair mats. For pets with long fur, mats are a never-ending problem. They not only look scruffy but also trap moisture next to the skin, making it easier for bacteria or parasites to thrive, says Dr. Hamil.

Hair mats are tricky to remove because the skin underneath is often tender. If you can convince your pet to hold still, you can often work out mats using a brush and comb. Or spray the mat with a detangler spray, available in pet supply stores. If the mat is too tight to remove or if it's right against the skin, you may have to clip it out with a pair of blunt scissors.

Trim the nails. Dogs' nails can grow surprisingly fast. If you don't trim them regularly, they are more likely to crack or tear.

Keep the teeth clean. Not very many people are dedicated enough to brush their dogs' teeth after every meal. But brushing them several times a week—or better yet, every day—

A weekly rubdown with a chamois is often enough to keep short-haired dogs' coats clean and healthy.

will help keep them clean and bacteria-free. More is involved than just cosmetics. Vets have found that the same bacteria in the mouth that cause gum disease can get into the bloodstream, possibly damaging the heart or other organs.

Dental care can be as intricate as using a toothbrush and paste made for dogs or as simple as wiping the outer surfaces of the teeth with a piece of gauze. Just giving dogs rawhide or rubber chews and hard biscuits to crunch will help keep the teeth clean.

Take care of the ears. The ears are naturally self-cleaning and don't require a lot of care. But you can periodically swab out the outer portions of the ears with a dry cotton ball. Or your vet may recommend using a combination ear cleaner and disinfectant. Don't use cotton swabs to clean out the ear canal, since this can push wax and debris in instead of getting it out.

Friends and Family

In years gone by, dogs kept busy hunting their prey and raising their young. Dogs today, on the other hand, often spend a lot of their time alone. Even if people are around, they don't have many opportunities to socialize with other dogs. This can lead to problems because dogs by nature are very social animals and they thrive on companionship, says Dr. Rupley. When they don't have a lot to do, they may get bored and depressed—and they may cope with these emotions by barking, digging holes in the yard, ripping plants out of the garden, or eating the furniture.

It's almost impossible to give dogs too many opportunities to socialize, Dr. Rupley adds. And the improvements in their behavior and overall moods are often dramatic. Making an effort to play with dogs for a half-hour or an hour a day will help keep them happy and energized. Better yet, take them out of the house and away from the neighborhood now and then. It's a happy dog who experiences new sights and new smells, and maybe a few other dogs to play with as well. And happy dogs are much less likely to be troublesome dogs, she explains.

NATURAL DEFENSES

The body has a marvelous system of defense, called the immune system, which protects against thousands of hazards, including bacteria, viruses, allergens, and even some snake and spider venoms—in short, anything in the environment that might pose a threat to health. When an invader, called an antigen, gets into the body, the immune system produces antibodies that fight the invasion. Once this immune response has been activated, the antibodies stay around in the body and provide a permanent defense against the antigen that triggered it.

Vaccination takes advantage of this defense mechanism by deliberately introducing a mild form of a disease—for example, rabies or distemper—into a dog's body. This stimulates the immune system to produce the antibodies that will provide permanent protection against more severe forms of the disease.

PART TWO

Symptoms and Solutions

Most dogs go through life without having major illnesses, but little things go wrong
all the time. Sometimes you'll need to see your veterinarian, but more often you'll be able
to take care of things at home by using simple and practical home remedies.

Aggression

Dogs act a lot differently among themselves than they do among people. Behavior that we would consider pushy or aggressive—shoving each other aside, growling, or snarling or snapping when they're annoyed—is part of their normal communication package. Dogs who are dominant and strong-willed use aggression to show their more passive and compliant mates that they're in charge and deserve respect. And any dog, even one who's normally shy and retiring, may get aggressive when the stakes are high enough, such as when there's a full bowl of food to protect.

"Some dogs are naturally aggressive at certain ages, such as when they're approaching

Dogs don't only display aggression when they're angry. This golden retriever and Staffordshire bull terrier mix are snarling and biting as part of a play-fight.

BREED SPECIFIC

Any dog can become aggressive under certain circumstances. But some breeds are more likely to be aggressive than others. English springer spaniels are prone to an inherited behavioral disorder called Rage Syndrome. Some American cocker spaniels may display unprovoked aggression. Other breeds that may have aggressive tendencies include Rottweilers, bullmastiffs, Akitas (left), Dobermans, and Chow Chows. These dogs can make excellent pets, but they generally need firm handling to keep their natural tendencies in check.

maturity," says Benjamin Hart, D.V.M., Ph.D., a veterinarian and professor of physiology and behavior at the School of Veterinary Medicine at the University of California at Davis. Males may be more aggressive than females because they're often more protective of territory, he adds. Females with litters, on the other hand, will do just about anything to protect their pups.

Even though aggression is entirely normal and acceptable among dogs, it's always a problem when it's directed toward people. "Fifty percent of all children under the age of 18 are bitten by a dog, usually one they know," says James M. Harris, D.V.M., medical director of Montclair Veterinary Clinic and Hospital in Oakland, Cal-

Seeing Eye to Eye

When the Stein family of Van Nuys, California, chose a year-old Akita named Radar at a shelter, they were eager to welcome him into their home.

To their dismay, though, on his first day in his new surroundings, Radar growled at their eight-year-old son, Ryan, when he kneeled down to look at his new dog.

"My husband and I were very scared because Radar was so big, and we had never had a dog that growled before," says Judy Stein. The Steins were sufficiently worried about the incident that they asked a professional trainer to take a look at Radar and at the way he and Ryan were interacting.

Almost instantly, the trainer saw something that Judy had missed: Ryan tended to kneel down when he wanted to play with Radar, and he also looked him right in the eye. Among dogs, a low body position means lower status, and Ryan was inadvertently giving Radar the idea that he didn't have to take the boy seriously. In addition, some dogs consider direct eye contact to be threatening, and Radar was responding in kind.

Apart from giving the Steins some general advice, such as keeping Radar and Ryan apart when the parents weren't there to supervise, the trainer recommended that Ryan always stand up tall when Radar was around, and not look him right in the eye.

The program worked from the start. Radar stopped feeling threatened, Ryan quit being scared, and the Steins all learned valuable lessons about getting along with dogs.

---

think they're in charge and that they have the right to tell their owners what to do.

The Usual Suspects

Lack of socialization. Animal behaviorists have discovered that puppies learn how to act around people and other pets most easily before 14 weeks of age. Dogs who are exposed to a wide range of people, places, and situations during this formative period grow up sure of themselves and at ease around others. Dogs who didn't have the benefit of these early experiences are more likely to be insecure, and insecure dogs tend to rely on scare tactics to resolve their problems, says Dr. Case-Pall.

Hormone fluctuations. "Unspayed female dogs can be hormonally affected before, during, or shortly after their estrus cycle," says Linda Goodloe, Ph.D., an animal behaviorist with practices in New York City and Philadelphia. Fluctuating hormone levels can make them unsociable and snappy for a few days, she explains.

Fear. Dogs sometimes bite in moments of panic—when someone comes up suddenly from behind, for example, or when they feel cornered and there's no way for them to escape. This is most common in dogs who have suffered in the past—due to bad handling from previous

---

ifornia. Even though most dogs will never seriously threaten their owners, aggression has a way of escalating if it isn't dealt with right away. Dogs who get away with grumbling may move on to snarling, growling, or worse.

More important, aggression toward people always means that dogs are unhappy, confused, or insecure, says Deena Case-Pall, Ph.D., a psychologist and animal behaviorist in Camarillo, California. At the very least it's a sign that they

Even friendly dogs may sometimes act aggressively when they have something they want to protect.

owners, for example, or even bad experiences with other dogs. Dogs have long memories and will sometimes act aggressively if they ever find themselves in a similarly frightening situation.

Pain. Dogs with arthritis, hip dysplasia, or any kind of illness or injury can get very crabby and will sometimes act aggressively when people get too close, says Dr. Harris. Their natural impulse is to go off and be by themselves until they're feeling better, and they'll sometimes protect their privacy by growling or biting.

Boredom. Just as children get bad-tempered when they don't have a lot going on, dogs sometimes get cranky when they're bored or under-stimulated, says Moira Cornell, a trainer in Canoga Park, California. Without regular exercise and mental excitement, dogs accumulate a lot of unused energy, and sometimes they channel that energy into aggressive behavior.

The Best Care

Broaden their horizons. Even though dogs do much of their learning when they're young, older dogs can also learn to be more easy-going and less fearful. Take your dog with you everywhere you can. When he's out in the world and experiencing different surroundings, he'll eventually get used to new noises and unfamiliar objects, and that will help make him feel more secure, says Dr. Case-Pall. Take along some small treats, too, and ask an obliging stranger to give him one. Meeting other people and dogs and realizing that they don't pose a threat will build his confidence, help him relax, and defuse any aggressive tendencies, says Cornell.

Reduce fear. When dogs are showing aggression because they're afraid, it's possible to desensitize them to the thing that they fear by gradually and gently increasing their exposure to it. If your dog wasn't raised around young children and is afraid of them, for example, walk him in public parks and around schoolyards. It will take some time before your dog realizes that they're no threat, but gradually he'll become more secure around them. Giving him a command to sit and stay when children are playing nearby will also build his confidence because it will earn him your praise for doing a good job.

Make time for play. Even dogs who are calm and sedate can build up tremendous amounts of energy during the day. Giving them a chance to vent their energy and blow off steam is often the best way to prevent aggression, says Wayne Hunthausen, D.V.M., an animal behaviorist in private practice in Westwood, Kansas, and co-author of *Practitioner's Guide to Pet*

Behavior Problems. Noncombative games such as Frisbee or fetching a ball are best. Jumping over a low bar or going through a play tunnel will also help channel their energy in acceptable ways. Whatever game or toy you choose, always keep control of it so that your dog never gets the chance to forget who's the leader.

Make him depend on you. Dogs who are aggressive once and get away with it are likely to get increasingly aggressive later on. It's probably not because they're bad-tempered, but because they feel they have the right to threaten people, explains Sandy Myers, a behavior consultant and trainer in Naperville, Illinois. You can turn things around by making sure they understand that you're the one they need to obey and please.

"Take every chance you can to assert your leadership," Myers says. "This reminds them that you're in charge." These little reminders don't have to be part of a formal training program, he adds. The idea is to incorporate into their days dozens of reminders that everything good in the world comes from people, and only when they're happy. Here are some suggestions.

CALL FOR HELP

No one gets too upset when a puppy gives a pint-size growl or a sleeping dog grumbles when someone disturbs him. But growls and grumbles have a way of graduating to bites, and that's why aggression is always a little scary, says Bonnie V. Beaver, D.V.M., professor and chief of medicine at the Texas Veterinary Medical Center at Texas A&M University in College Station.

A big, strong dog can exert about 1,200 crushing pounds per inch of bite pressure. A 160-pound man, by contrast, can exert about 65 pounds. Veterinarians advise getting help at the first sign of problems. Your vet will want to make sure there isn't a physical problem that's making your dog quick to bite. At the same time, she'll create a program that will help your dog understand that being aggressive toward people is never appropriate behavior.

- At meal times, have your dog sit or lie down and wait before he's fed. Then put his bowl on the floor and tell him it's okay to eat.
- Get out the leash, but don't put it on him until he sits or stands calmly.
- Open the door to go outside, but only let him out when he sits, waits politely, or follows some other command.

Dogs who get regular obedience training respect their owners' leadership and are less likely to feel the need to act aggressively.

21

Appetite Loss

It's natural for dogs' appetites to fluctuate, not only with the seasons, but at different stages of life. Puppies usually have voracious appetites—for dog food, cat food, or anything else they can reach. Dogs in their senior years, on the other hand, usually eat less because they're not as active as they used to be and because their sense of smell has faded, making food less appetizing.

Every dog needs a different amount of food, so you can't measure a dog's health by how much goes into—or disappears from—the food bowl. Veterinarians are more interested in changes in a dog's usual habits. A dog who normally eats like a horse and then suddenly turns his nose up at his food is probably sick or at least a little depressed, says Kris Ellingsen, D.V.M., a veterinarian in private practice in Portland, Oregon.

There are probably dozens of reasons dogs may suddenly start eating less. Here are the most common.

The Usual Suspects

They're eating somewhere else. People usually suspect their dogs are sick when they quit eating, but sometimes they reject their own dinner because they've found another source of food that they like better. "If your dog refuses his usual dry kibble, but gorges on the cat's food, we don't worry as much as if he turns his nose up at every tasty treat," says

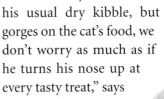

When dogs suddenly start rejecting their favorite brand of food, it may be because the manufacturer has changed the recipe.

CALL FOR HELP

Veterinarians always worry when dogs quit eating for more than a day or two because there are dozens of physical problems, some of them quite serious, that can make them lose their interest in food. Cancer often causes appetite loss. So do problems with the pancreas, liver, or kidneys. Even heart disease can cause dogs to eat less because there may be accumulations of fluids in the chest cavity.

You don't have to rush to the veterinarian when your pet misses a meal or two, says Craig N. Carter, D.V.M., Ph.D., head of epidemiology at the Texas Veterinary Medical Diagnostic Laboratory at Texas A&M University in College Station. If the appetite doesn't come back fairly quickly, however, you'll want to talk to your vet.

Rance Sellon, D.V.M., a veterinarian specializing in internal medicine at Washington State University in Pullman.

Gum or tooth problems. Dogs who have gum infections or a broken tooth will often start eating less because it's painful for them to chew, says Deborah C. Mallu, D.V.M., a veterinarian in private practice in Sedona, Arizona.

Changes in cuisine. It's not uncommon for dogs to happily gobble the same food every day for 10 years without ever losing their enthusiasm, and then one day turn up their noses in distaste. "Pet food companies periodically make changes to their recipes," says Taylor Wallace, D.V.M., a veterinarian in private practice in Seattle. Even when dogs are perfectly satisfied with their chow, owners sometimes decide to switch brands or flavors. If your dog dislikes the food, he's not going to eat it.

Changes in routine. Dogs crave predictability, and even small changes in their lives can upset them so much that they lose their appetites, says Dr. Wallace. This usually happens when the household is in a bit of an uproar—during a move to a new house, for example, or when friends and relatives start congregating around the holidays. "Some dogs stop eating when their owners go away on vacation," Dr. Wallace says. "Hunger won't matter to them if they're missing their owners that much."

Distractions. Even though most dogs can focus on food to the exclusion of everything else, others don't care about eating all that much and will wander away from their food bowls at the slightest distraction, says Agnes Rupley, D.V.M., a veterinarian in private practice in College Station, Texas. "More interesting occupations, such as barking at the neighboring cat or monitoring the birdbath, may entice your dog away from his food bowl," she explains.

A Taste for Trash

PUPPY DOG TALES

Alaskan malamutes aren't known for their diminutive appetites. Most of the time they stuff themselves silly, and Mako was no exception. He would gobble everything that went into his bowl, then eagerly look around for more. But then something strange started happening. His owner, Heather Forte, an artist in Camano Island, Washington, began noticing that one day a week, on Fridays, Mako wouldn't eat a thing. The rest of the week, however, his appetite was the same as it had always been.

Heather was mystified by these end-of-the-week culinary doldrums—until one Thursday night when she saw the neighbors taking their trash out to the curb. All of a sudden, Heather had a very good idea what was probably happening.

The next morning, she let Mako out in the backyard for his morning relief and then watched closely from the kitchen window. She saw Mako walk to the gate, pop open the latch, and meander out into the street. Heather hurried around to the front window, just in time to see Mako tip over the garbage can and begin pawing off the lid.

While Heather was delighted by Mako's ingenuity, she wasn't thrilled with the object of his attentions. So she took quick action—and a week later Mako discovered a padlock on the gate. And that Friday night, Heather was pleased to notice, he had no trouble at all finishing his supper.

Illness. Dogs who are sick almost always lose their appetites, says Dr. Sellon. Usually the problem is minor—a sore throat, a fever, or a bit of joint pain—and they'll resume their usual diets once they're feeling better. But dogs also lose their appetites when they have more serious conditions, so it's best to call your vet if your dog has gone two days or more without food.

The Best Care

Test his appetite. It's hard to tell whether dogs have truly lost their appetites or whether they're merely bored with what they're eating. One way to find out is to put several different foods in front of them—chicken-flavored baby food, for example, along with liverwurst or canned food. If your dog starts eating one or more of the treats with his old enthusiasm, you'll know that taste, not appetite, is the issue,

When this shar-pei goes off his food, his owner tempts him to eat again by coddling him and feeding him baby food by hand.

says Karen Overall, V.M.D., Ph.D., head of the behavior clinic at the University of Pennsylvania School of Veterinary Medicine in Philadelphia.

Pamper his emotions. Dogs occasionally get depressed and anxious, and when they're feeling bad, they're very likely to lose their appetites, says Dr. Rupley. "If he seems to be interested in food, but won't eat, try sitting with him or feeding by hand," she suggests. "Petting can stimulate eating in some dogs," she adds.

FAST FIX Dogs who are bored with their usual dry food will often perk up if you add a spoonful of canned food and some warm water to create a saucy mix.

Make every bite count. Even though it's safe for dogs to go without food for a day or two, dogs who have a reduced appetite for a long time may fall short in vital nutrients. Veterinarians supply prescription diets that are dense in nutrients, low in filler, and easier to digest than commercial foods. Or you may want to try supplementing your dog's usual food with healthful leftovers such as lean chicken or beef.

Encourage him to drink. "Dogs who aren't eating may not be drinking enough either," says Dr. Ellingsen. Dogs won't drink extra water on command, but they'll usually lap up more flavorful liquids, such as chicken soup, broth, or tuna juice diluted with a little water.

Bad Breath

When dogs have bad breath, it means that something's not right either in the mouth itself or internally. Although a healthy dog's breath will be warmer and moister than human breath, it shouldn't smell bad.

"Your dog's breath might not smell all that sweet, but it shouldn't be too noticeable either," says Paul Cleland, D.V.M., a veterinarian specializing in animal dental health in Fort Collins, Colorado.

The Usual Suspects

Periodontal disease. The main cause of bad breath in dogs is periodontal disease, an infection of the gums. It's caused by poor dental hygiene. Bacteria and saliva in the mouth attack food fragments stuck between the gums and the teeth and produce a slightly sticky film of decaying material called plaque that clings to the teeth. If it's not cleaned off, it hardens into a brownish deposit called tartar. The tartar wedges itself between the teeth and gums and eats away the tissue and bone that hold the teeth in place.

Periodontal disease affects as many as 85 percent of dogs over three years of age. Dogs lose many more teeth from periodontal disease than from any other cause, including cavities and broken teeth. As well as causing bad breath, untreated periodontal disease can cause infections

OPEN WIDE

Brushing a dog's teeth doesn't take a lot of time. One simple way is to turn your finger into a toothbrush with a finger brush, available from pet stores and veterinarians. Use a toothpaste formulated for dogs because the frothing ingredient in human toothpastes can upset a dog's stomach. Canine toothpastes come in the meaty flavors that dogs like.

Hold a small dog in your lap, or sit on the floor with a larger dog. Place the finger brush between the cheek and gums and rub gently up and down, being sure to reach right to the back teeth.

Most dogs will let you hold their mouths open with one hand and rub with the other to clean their inner tooth surfaces.

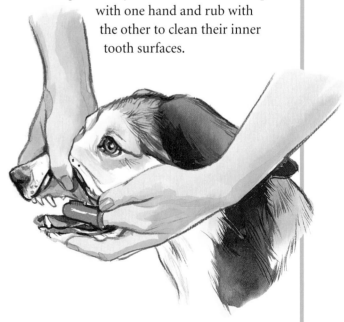

that get into the bloodstream and may lead to heart and kidney problems.

Indigestion. When the teeth and gums are in good health, bad breath may be due to poor digestion, says Ehud Sela, D.V.M., a veterinarian in private practice near Fort Lauderdale, Florida. Dogs often get indigestion from eating fatty foods such as pork or table scraps. They also get it from eating too much too fast.

Internal problems. Dogs whose breath smells like urine may have kidney problems, says Tim Banker, D.V.M., a veterinarian in private practice in Greensboro, North Carolina. Normally the kidneys purify the blood by getting rid of waste products, but if they're not functioning properly, the waste builds up in the bloodstream and causes bad breath. A sweet, "fruity" smell, on the other hand, could be the result of too much sugar in the bloodstream, caused by diabetes. And a strong, foul smell might indicate liver disease.

Crunching a raw carrot every couple of days helps keep this boxer's teeth and gums in great shape.

CALL FOR HELP

Once plaque has hardened into tartar, it's time to visit the veterinary dentist. Tartar is hard to scrape off and, as long as it stays in place, it's causing damage under the gum line. "Periodontal disease should be treated early because once it has progressed to an advanced level, treatment of any kind may be less effective," says Jean Hawkins, D.V.M., a veterinarian in private practice in Boise, Idaho.

The Best Care

Encourage dogs to chew. The best defense against bad breath caused by plaque and tartar is chewing. This is especially important for dogs who are fed only soft foods and miss out on the chewing and scraping action that gets rid of plaque, says Dr. Banker.

Most dogs love chewing, so it's just a matter of finding the right things for them to chew. A rawhide or Nylabone chew toy will provide hours of fun as well as healthy teeth and gums. Crunching up dog biscuits and dry foods will give teeth a good scrape. Demolishing a raw carrot every couple of days will scrub plaque away and provide fiber and vitamins A and C as a bonus. And the tendons of a cooked oxtail will help "floss" the teeth, getting into hard-to-reach crevices, says Dr. Banker.

Brush regularly. "Start cleaning your dog's teeth as early as two months of age," recommends Dr. Sela. "The puppy's milk teeth are going to fall out, but in the meantime, she'll be

DOGGY DENTISTRY

You won't come across a dog with a set of false teeth in a glass of water next to his basket, but it's not unknown for dogs to need tooth repair. Dogs often lose or damage teeth through accidents, bad nutrition, or chewing things that are too hard. When a dog's tooth is damaged, but can be salvaged, a veterinary dentist will repair the tooth with a crown, says Kenneth Lyon, D.V.M., a veterinary dental specialist in private practice in Mesa, Arizona. The crown will look and function just like a natural tooth and will also help protect what's left of the dog's real tooth.

Another way of saving a damaged or broken tooth is to rebuild it with an acrylic composite ceramic that is bonded to the tooth with a substance that goes rockhard when exposed to ultraviolet light. And in some cases, dogs really do need dentures, which can be surgically implanted in the jawbone. This is usually done for valuable show, police, and security dogs, who always need to look—or bite—their best, says Dr Lyon.

One such dog is Moose, the Jack Russell terrier who stars as Eddie on the television show *Frasier*. His teeth are his fortune, so when they started to give him trouble, Dr. Lyon was summoned to the rescue. Moose needed seven root canal treatments if his teeth—and his career—were to be saved, says Dr. Lyon. The treatment was successful, and Moose remained a TV star.

getting used to having her teeth brushed." Start very gently, rubbing just a couple of teeth at a time with a fingertip moistened with chicken or beef broth. You'll soon be able to graduate to a proper brushing with canine toothpaste.

Prevent indigestion. Dogs who eat rich or fatty foods or suddenly change their diets may get digestive problems that can cause bad breath, says Dr. Sela.

FAST FIX There are several brands of mouthwashes for dogs. They contain an active ingredient called stabilized chlorine deoxide, which is activated by the warmth of the mouth. It breaks down the sulfur by-products that are made by bacteria in the mouth. Always use a mouthwash formulated for pets; most human ones contain too much alcohol to be safe for dogs.

BREED SPECIFIC

Toy breeds such as Maltese, Yorkshire terriers, and poodles are especially prone to bad teeth and gums. All dogs have the same number of teeth, but small dogs' teeth are often over-crowded, providing more crevices to trap food particles and provide footholds for tartar.

Barking

According to the Occupational Health and Safety Act, 90 decibels is the maximum safe level for noise. Jackhammers exceed this volume. So do sirens and car alarms. And, as many irate home owners can attest, so do the barking dogs next door.

From a human viewpoint, persistent barking is among the most obnoxious misbehaviors that dogs indulge in. Dogs have a different perspective. Barking is one of their ways of communicating, and just as some people talk a lot, some dogs bark a lot. "Most dogs bark for a reason, but sometimes only they know what it is," says David S. Spiegel, V.M.D., a veterinarian in private practice in Wilmington, Delaware, who specializes in canine behavior problems.

Barking isn't merely a form of canine chat, however. Dogs who bark so long and so loud that they make themselves hoarse are usually unhappy or feeling threatened by something. Barking is their way of dispelling tension—and asking for help.

The Usual Suspects

Boredom. It's normal for dogs to bark once or twice when they want their owners' attention. Dogs who keep barking, or who bark even when they're alone and nothing's going on, however, are probably bored. Barking expresses their frustration and helps keep them occupied, explains Jill Yorey,

training coordinator for the Society for the Prevention of Cruelty to Animals in Los Angeles.

Territorial instincts. Dogs have a natural instinct to protect their surroundings and will bark when strangers, human or animal, approach their territory. "Dogs don't bark to scare away people, but to tell others in the family that something is approaching," says Susanne B. Johnson, Ph.D., a behaviorist in private practice in Beaverdam, Virginia.

Fear. A dog's hearing is about four times more sensitive than a human's, so sounds we take for granted, like the roar of a garbage truck, can scare them half to death—and scared dogs bark.

BREED SPECIFIC

Small dogs such as Pomeranians and Yorkshire terriers have reputations for being big barkers. One reason they're so vocal, experts believe, is that they know their small size makes them hard for people (or other dogs) to see. Barking is their way of saying, "I'm down here, watch what you're doing." In addition, dogs who have been bred to be watchful, such as bearded collies (left) and cocker spaniels, also tend to be vocal, says Robert J. Garcia, D.V.M., a veterinarian in private practice in San Jose, California.

Separation anxiety. Dogs who are very fearful or insecure may panic whenever their owners leave the house. One way of coping—in addition to such things as destroying furnishings or jumping out of windows—is to bark, sometimes for a half-hour or more. "If a dog is left alone too much when he's young, he may develop a habit of making a fuss about it that extends into adulthood," says Susan E. Anderson, D.V.M., a clinical instructor of outpatient medicine in the department of small animal clinical sciences at the University of Florida College of Veterinary Medicine in Gainesville.

The Best Care

Give them permission to bark. It sounds paradoxical, but dogs who bark a lot will usually quit it once their owners teach them to bark— and, later, to be quiet—on command, says Kathy Marmack, a trainer at the San Diego Zoo.

The first part is easy. Do something that you know makes your dog bark. Jump up and down. Act excited. Wave his favorite toy around. Open the food cabinet. Whatever it takes, get him barking—then praise him and say "Good bark!" when he lets loose. If you keep this up for several days, practicing five minutes each day, most dogs will quickly learn to bark when you tell them to, says Marmack.

Once dogs know how to bark on command, they can also learn to stop. Start by using the command that gets them barking. Then, during a pause between barks, hand over a treat and say "Good quiet!" Keep practicing until your dog always stops barking when you give the "quiet" command. Teaching dogs these commands lets

Some dogs bark because they've learned that it gets them what they want. One way to stop persistent barkers is to reward them only for silence, not noise.

them do the barking they naturally want to do, while at the same time ensuring that you get some peace now and then.

Bark back. Dogs dislike loud noises, which is why many trainers recommend blowing an air horn or banging two pan lids together whenever they start barking. Once dogs get the idea that their barking invariably is followed by some horrible sound, they'll learn to be a little quieter, says Tony Bugarin, a trainer in Los Angeles.

It's best to make the noises when you're standing behind your dog or are otherwise out of sight, Bugarin adds. You want your dog to be startled, but you don't want him to associate you with things he dislikes.

Try a citronella collar. Habitual barkers will often stop when they've been fitted with a citronella collar. These are specialized collars that emit a quick spritz of citronella—a plant extract with a smell dogs dislike—at the sound of barking. "Citronella collars are effective about 70 percent of the time," says Linda Goodloe, Ph.D., a certified applied animal behaviorist with practices in New York City and Philadelphia.

Keep them busy. Dogs who are playing, eating, or generally having a good time are much less likely to indulge in monotonous barking than those who are bored and frustrated. The challenge is that nonstop barking usually occurs when owners are gone, which means no one's around to keep them entertained. The solution, says Deena Case-Pall, Ph.D., a psychologist and animal behaviorist in Camarillo, California, is to provide amusements they can do on their own. Many trainers recommend giving dogs hollow toys such as Buster Cubes or Kongs, which can be loaded with food. Dogs will happily spend hours trying to get at the treats inside, and busy dogs usually aren't barking dogs.

Giving dogs a lot of exercise will also curtail the need to bark, says Moira Cornell, a trainer in Canoga Park, California. It's especially good to take them for walks in the morning before you leave the house. This will tire them out a bit and also allow them to burn off some of the energy that they normally use for barking.

Reduce their fears. Dogs are just as likely as people to be afraid of different things and situations—and to get less afraid the more they're exposed to them. Dogs who bark because they're easily frightened will often become more secure, and quieter, when their owners gradually expose them to the things or situations that they dislike, says Cornell. A dog who barks because he's unfamiliar with children, for example, may get calmer if you take him for frequent walks around school playgrounds or neighborhood parks, places where he'll meet lots of children and discover they're not a threat. As long as your dog acts calmly—around children, vacuum cleaners, or whatever else he's afraid of—praise him for being good, she explains. When he barks, either ignore it or remove him from the situation—but don't reward him. The combination of familiarity and rewards is very effective at helping dogs get more confident as well as quieter. This type of training, called desensitization, works best when it's done slowly over a period of weeks or even months, adds Cornell. It's not a process you can rush because that makes dogs more nervous, she explains.

It's possible to desensitize dogs to sounds that make them bark by gradually increasing their exposure to them. This papillon mix is getting used to the hairdryer, with the help of some treats and praise.

Trespassers Beware

When Muncie, an eight-year-old Rottweiler, gives a particular kind of bark, her owners, James and Julia Rainey, sit up and take notice. Their house in Glenrowan, Victoria, Australia, borders bush that's home to some dangerous creepy-crawlies—and when one of them comes calling, Muncie lets everyone know. So far she's alerted the family to a huge centipede, a scorpion, and two snakes. Her method is to circle the creature, giving a distinctive growly bark, until a family member comes to investigate. Her most impressive victim was an aggressive and potentially lethal five-foot-long brown snake. Muncie had bitten 18 inches off its tail by the time Julia arrived.

"She's always looking out for us," says James. "When I go away, it gives me great peace of mind to know that Muncie's home, watching out for my family."

You can use this same technique to help dogs with separation anxiety, says Sandy Myers, a behavior consultant and trainer in Naperville, Illinois. Essentially, what you'll do is "practice" leaving. On a weekend when you're going to be home all day, act as though you're getting ready to leave the house—but don't leave. Pick up your keys, rattle them, then put them down and sit down for a while. Then rattle them again. Or open the door and close it. By repeating some of the rituals that precede leaving, but not actually going out, your dog will slowly begin to attach less importance to them, Myers explains.

Once your dog is a little more comfortable with the pre-departure rituals, try going out the door, Myers says. Step outside, close the door, then come right back in again before your dog has a chance to react. As long as he's calm, give him a treat and some praise. Then go out the door again and come back in. Give him another treat. Keep doing this until he's getting more and more relaxed. Then try staying outside for longer—it may be only a few seconds at first. As long as your dog is calm when you come back in, keep giving him praise and treats. Most dogs will get more and more relaxed about the whole process. As their anxiety diminishes, so will their barking, Myers says.

Give them more attention than they asked for. Attention-seeking barkers will sometimes quit the noise when they learn that it results in work. "Tell him to sit or lie down," says Benjamin Hart, D.V.M., Ph.D., a veterinarian and professor of physiology and behavior at the University of California School of Veterinary Medicine at Davis. "Eventually, he'll stop being so demanding."

Reward silence, not noise. Many dogs bark because they've learned that it works: They get let outside, they get the treat, or they get the attention. Essentially, they're being rewarded for being noisy. "To stop the barking, wait for a pause in the noise. Only then give your dog what he wants," says Dr. Hart. "You want to reward him for being quiet, not loud."

FAST FIX Neutering or spaying will decrease barking in about 50 percent of cases, says Robert J. Garcia, D.V.M., a veterinarian in private practice in San Jose, California. Neutering often reduces dogs' territorial instincts and, with it, their barking.

Black Specks in Fur

During the warm months, dogs sometimes take on a grainy appearance, as though they've been sprinkled with pepper. It looks like they're badly in need of a bath, but the true cause is more troublesome than a little dirt.

The Usual Suspects

Fleas. Dogs with a peppery appearance are infested with fleas. Those black specks are the wastes that fleas leave behind. The reason they're so dark is that the blood that makes up the fleas' diet becomes dark once it is digested.

To check for fleas, brush your dog over a piece of white paper (left). Then use a damp cotton ball to pick up the debris that's been shed (below). Any flea dirt will dissolve, leaving a brownish stain.

Dogs with fleas will invariably do a lot of scratching or biting at the skin. The rump around the base of the tail is likely to be where they concentrate their efforts, but dogs with fleas sometimes itch all over, especially if they're allergic to flea saliva. Flea-bite allergy is the most common allergy among dogs, and even a single flea bite can be tremendously itchy. What causes the allergic reaction is an anticoagulant in the saliva that keeps the blood liquid so that the flea can feast on it.

The adult fleas that bite and cause so much misery make up only about 2 percent of the flea population. The rest is divided among the egg, larval, and cocoon stages. While adult fleas are fairly easy to kill, those in the cocoon stage are impervious to insecticides and can survive in the most extreme conditions. That's why fleas are so hard to get rid off. No matter how many adult fleas you dispatch, there are always plenty more to take their place.

Fleas are mainly a seasonal problem, although in the age of central heating they can thrive all year. What usually happens is that flea cocoons lie dormant in carpets and upholstery through much of the winter, then suddenly become active in the spring. Dogs with flea allergies get so itchy that they'll go on scratching much longer than they would just from the flea bite. Often the bitten area doesn't have a chance to heal because of the constant scratching, so the only way to stop the scratching is to eliminate the fleas.

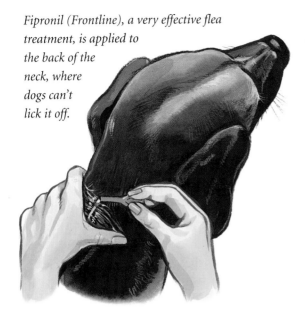

Fipronil (Frontline), a very effective flea treatment, is applied to the back of the neck, where dogs can't lick it off.

The Best Care

Stop fleas from multiplying. Fleas can multiply at staggering rates. "During the six weeks or so of her life span, an adult female flea lays as many as 2,000 tiny, slippery eggs. These fall or are brushed off into carpets and soft furnishings, where they develop into larvae and then cocoons, ready to spring to life as adult fleas the moment the air temperature is high enough," explains Bernadine Cruz, D.V.M., a veterinarian in private practice in Laguna Hills, California. This means that the only effective way to get rid of fleas is to interrupt their reproductive cycles.

Many vets recommend a prescription medication called lufenuron (Program) for dogs in flea-ridden areas. Given monthly as a pill, it circulates in the dog's bloodstream and is ingested by fleas when they feed, explains Dr.

Cruz. Once it's inside the flea, lufenuron stops the eggs from developing into adults, so breaking the lifecycle.

Another successful weapon in the flea war is fipronil (Frontline). Available in pet supply stores and from veterinarians, it's applied as a liquid to the back of a dog's neck where she can't lick it off. "It gets into the oil layer of the skin and travels from one hair follicle to the next. Within 24 hours, it will spread from the tip of the nose to the tip of the tail," says Dr. Cruz. Frontline is very safe for dogs and around children, because the fipronil isn't absorbed into their bodies. Once it's in the hair follicles, it stays active for 30 to 90 days, says Dr. Cruz.

In areas where fleas are a major problem, Frontline can be used in conjunction with Program, says Dr. Cruz. Program interrupts the lifecycle and Frontline kills any adults that migrate from other pets or from outside.

Try a powder. While it's not a quick cure, a chemical called sodium polyborate (Rx for

CALL FOR HELP

Within just a few weeks, a heavy infestation of fleas can remove enough blood from a puppy's body to cause a serious loss of blood, resulting in anemia, says Bernadine Cruz, D.V.M., a veterinarian in private practice in Laguna Hills, California. To check for anemia, look at your dog's gums, which should be bright pink. Pale or muddy-looking gums could mean anemia, and you'll want to take your dog to the vet.

PROTECTION FROM THE INSIDE

Even though flea-control medications are very safe and effective, many people are reluctant to give their dogs drugs all year. One drug-free way to make fleas less troublesome is to provide top nutrition. "For a lot of dogs I've seen with flea problems, a high-quality diet has worked really well," says Susan Wynn, D.V.M., a veterinarian at Emory University in Atlanta and co-editor of *Complementary and Alternative Veterinary Medicine.*

"Look for a substantial amount of good-quality protein very high up in the label ingredients—chicken, turkey, beef, lamb, fish, or eggs." Dr. Wynn recommends premium foods such as Innova, Pet Guard, and Nutro. Any diet can be improved by adding equal quantities of lean meats and vegetables, making sure they make up about 30 percent of the total diet.

Fleas) provides a kind of environmental shield against fleas, says Susan Wynn, D.V.M., a veterinarian at Emory University in Atlanta and co-editor of *Complementary and Alternative Veterinary Medicine.* Once a year, work the fine powder into your carpets and your pet's bedding, says Dr. Wynn. It's easy to do as long as you're prepared for a lot of dusty work. Or call in a professional company such as Fleabusters.

Suck fleas up. Most flea eggs wind up on carpets and upholstery, says Dr. Cruz. To stop a new generation of fleas from taking hold, vacuum the house thoroughly and wash your pet's bedding once a week, she says.

Wash them away. The quickest way to get rid of adult fleas is to wash dogs with a medicated shampoo, preferably one containing a natural flea-control ingredient called pyrethrins. Flea shampoos kill adult fleas on contact, and simply washing dogs will flush others down the drain, says Tim Banker, D.V.M., a veterinarian in private practice in Greensboro, North Carolina. Shampoos have no effect on flea eggs and larvae, however, so they need to be used every couple of weeks as fleas mature into adults.

Comb them out. Daily grooming with a flea comb is an easy and effective way to remove both fleas and their eggs. After each stroke, dip the comb in soapy water to kill the fleas, says Dr. Wynn. Then flush both the water and the fleas down the drain to get rid of them for good.

Regular combing helps keep this Maltese's coat flea-free. After each stroke, the comb is dipped into soapy water to kill fleas and eggs that are picked up.

Bleeding

The sight of blood makes many people queasy, but bleeding isn't usually serious enough to be a real problem. And there's rarely a mystery about what caused it. Even dogs who spend most of their time indoors will occasionally get cuts—usually on the paw pads or around the mouth when they bite on something sharp.

Even small cuts can bleed a lot, although bleeding usually slows within a few minutes. More serious is blood that keeps flowing, either because the wound is serious or because a dog has a medical problem that interferes with normal clotting. Wounds that don't bleed can also be worrisome because bleeding is one of nature's ways of flushing away germs. Wounds that are so narrow that they don't bleed much are often the ones that get infected.

The Usual Suspects

Cuts. Bleeding is nearly always caused by minor cuts. Dogs who cut their feet on broken glass can bleed a lot, partly because of the force of gravity, and also because dogs don't put their feet up when they're injured—they keep running around, which makes wounds slow to heal. Cuts that are less than an inch long and not too deep will usually heal on their own. Larger cuts may need stitches. "Areas where wounds often don't heal well include the paw pads, the joints, and around the groin," says Suann Hosie, D.V.M., a veterinarian in private practice in Vancouver, British Columbia, Canada.

CALL FOR HELP

Bleeding that doesn't stop quickly means your dog could be in trouble—either because a major artery has been cut or because he has a medical problem that's interfering with the body's ability to heal. He needs to see a veterinarian right away.

Compared to veins, arteries are high-pressure systems, which makes their bleeding harder to control. Veins that are cut usually ooze for a bit, then stop. Arteries that are cut can bleed heavily, often in little spurts, says Lillian Roberts, D.V.M., a veterinarian in private practice in Palm Desert, California.

Some dogs have medical problems that interfere with the blood's clotting ability. Even small wounds can go on bleeding for a long time. And some household poisons, mainly rodent baits, contain ingredients that inhibit clotting and may cause unexplained bleeding from the nose or other soft tissues.

Bites. These are among the most dangerous wounds, even though there often isn't much bleeding. Bites are often narrow and deep, creating a safe haven for bacteria.

Cat bites tend to be the worst because their saliva is packed with germs and the wounds are exceedingly narrow. Dogs with serious cat bites should always be treated by a veterinarian, says Dr. Hosie.

The Best Care

Apply pressure. The first priority is always to stop the bleeding. "Apply direct pressure on the wound with a clean cloth," says John Angus, D.V.M., a veterinarian in private practice in Mesa, Arizona.

If blood seeps through, don't remove the cloth because that will break up the clot that is trying to form. Just pack another cloth on top of the first one and maintain the pressure, advises Dr. Angus.

Clean it. The biggest risk from most wounds isn't the bleeding itself, but the infection that may follow. And once bacteria get inside a wound and start multiplying, it can be a challenge to get them out. That's why it's essential to clean wounds as soon as the bleeding has stopped.

Wash the area very thoroughly with soap and warm water, says Dr. Angus. Don't take shortcuts. Less than several minutes washing the wound is probably not enough.

Pat the wound dry with a clean cloth or a gauze pad. Don't use cotton balls because the fibers will get into the wound.

Douse the area with an over-the-counter antiseptic solution such as Betadine. "Don't use alcohol because it will cause an extremely painful sting," says Dr. Angus.

GIVING FIRST-AID

Dogs with cut arteries can lose tremendous amounts of blood in a hurry. Don't wait until you get to your veterinarian's to stop the bleeding. Immediately press firmly on the wound—preferably with a clean cloth, although your hand is fine if nothing else is available. If this doesn't help, you'll need to work on the pressure points.

Pressure points are areas where major arteries are close to the surface of the skin. Pressing against these spots with your fingers reduces the amount of blood flowing through the arteries. The main pressure points are located in the armpits, in the groin, and just below the base of the tail.

Go for the pressure point closest to the wound, between the wound and the heart, and press firmly with your three middle fingers until the bleeding slows down.

It's important to relax the pressure for a few seconds every five minutes to make sure some blood gets through to keep the nerves and muscle tissue in the injured area alive.

Thoroughly cleaning wounds with soap and water will help prevent bacteria from getting established. Veterinarians usually recommend washing wounds for at least three to five minutes.

Blood in Stool

Blood is the last thing anyone wants to see in stools because it can be a warning sign of cancer, at least in people. Dogs can get intestinal cancer, too, but that's usually not what the blood means. Most of the time, in fact, dogs with blood in their stools aren't especially sick and will quickly get better with the right treatment.

It's not always easy to see blood in the stools, adds Bonnie Wilcox, D.V.M., a veterinarian in private practice in Preemption, Illinois. Sometimes it's visible right on the surface, but it can also be mixed in, making the stools look dark and tarry rather than bloody.

You can safely ignore one or two bloody stools if things get back to normal in a day or two. Blood that keeps showing up needs to be checked out by a veterinarian, Dr. Wilcox says.

The Usual Suspects

Parasites. Blood in the stools may be a sign of whipworms, parasites that take up residence in the colon and cause irritation and bleeding. Blood caused by whipworms is usually on the surface of the stools and will appear quite red.

Hookworms, on the other hand, usually cause stools to look tarry. This is because hookworms live farther up in the digestive tract in the small intestine. Blood that originates in the small intestine gets partially digested, causing it to turn black before it leaves the body in the stools. Hookworms are more of a problem than whipworms because they can extract large amounts of blood and essential nutrients, making dogs weak and constantly tired.

Infections. Any infection in the intestinal tract may cause irritation and bleeding. Dogs who eat raw or spoiled food or dead wildlife sometimes get bacterial infections, which are readily treated with antibiotics.

Viral infections such as flu can also cause bloody stools, including bloody diarrhea. There isn't a cure for flu, but most viral infections clear up on their own in a week or two.

Sharp objects. Dogs will chew and swallow just about anything. A piece of cardboard, a child's building block, or a stick in the wood pile will all pass the taste test, as far as they're concerned. Dogs' digestive tracts were designed for

Hedges and bushes are full of smells that dogs find fascinating—but those smells may be coming from things that could play havoc with their digestive systems, causing bloody stools.

CALL FOR HELP

Dogs often have mild intestinal problems, and for the most part they get over them just fine. Things are different for puppies, however. Their systems aren't strong enough to handle intestinal or stomach upheavals, and because of their small sizes they can't afford to lose any blood. "If there's abundant blood in the stools, or if it accompanies diarrhea, that's an emergency for a puppy," says Christine Wilford, D.V.M., a veterinarian in private practice in Edmonds, Washington.

indiscriminate eating, but even so they may bleed a bit when something scrapes the lining of the large intestine on the way out.

Large objects. It doesn't happen often, but sometimes dogs swallow objects that are too big to pass through their systems. This causes the intestines to strain and keep straining, which can cause bloody diarrhea. The only solution may be for a veterinarian to reach in—by hand or surgically—to remove the obstruction, says Dr. Wilcox.

Changes in diet. Considering the strange things that they eat, dogs have surprisingly sensitive stomachs when it comes to changing diets. Switching to a new food will sometimes cause the stomach to heave and churn in protest,

When you take your dog hiking, bring water from home so he doesn't need to drink "wild" water that might be contaminated.

which may damage small blood vessels near its surface, causing substantial bleeding.

The Best Care

Put them on a day-long fast. Since bleeding is often caused by nothing worse than an irritating bout of diarrhea, veterinarians often recommend putting dogs on a fast for 24 hours. This gives the stomach and intestines time to recover from whatever's causing the upset, says Dr. Wilcox. "When the diarrhea clears up, the blood usually clears up, too," she says. Fasting dogs still need to drink, however, so make sure they have access to plenty of fresh water.

Dogs can safely go for a few days without food, but don't wait longer than a day if the bleeding continues, Dr. Wilcox adds. Make an appointment with your veterinarian and get it checked out right away.

Take care of the worms. Worms are easy to treat with the proper medicines, says Dr. Wilcox. Dogs who live in areas where hookworms are

common are often given monthly doses of pyrantel pamoate, an over-the-counter preventive medicine. Reducing your dog's exposure to parasites is probably the best way to stop bleeding. One way to do this is simply to stop dogs from sniffing (or worse, eating) other pets' stools. "Parasites easily spread when they sniff droppings," says Christine Wilford, D.V.M., a veterinarian in private practice in Edmonds,

Washington. Removing stools from the yard every day will also help ensure that dogs don't reinfect themselves later on.

Water can also be a problem because many waterways are breeding grounds for parasites. If you live near "wild" water or take your dog hiking, you can prevent problems by keeping him away from natural sources of water and only giving him water that you bring from home.

COLLECTING A STOOL SAMPLE

When people first discover blood in their dogs' stools, they're understandably a little nervous, which is why they often rush their dogs to the veterinarian without doing the one thing that would make everyone's life a little easier: collect a stool sample.

No one enjoys picking up dog droppings, but your veterinarian will need a sample to make the diagnosis, says Christine Wilford, D.V.M., a veterinarian in private practice in Edmonds, Washington. You don't have to grab the whole thing—just a small piece is fine, Dr. Wilford adds.

To collect a stool sample, pick it up with a Pooper Scooper, then transfer the contents to a plastic bag. Or put a plastic bag over your hand and pick up the sample. Roll the bag off your hand, flipping it so the sample is on the inside. Wrap the sample tightly in the plastic to keep air out, and take it with you when you take your dog in for his checkup, says Dr. Wilford. It's best to pick a

sample that's just a few hours old, she adds. If you aren't able to get to your vet right away, it's fine to refrigerate the sample, Dr. Wilford says. But don't keep it longer than eight hours. "Many people bring in rock-hard, days-old samples, which are pretty much useless," she says. "The sample must be examined while it's still soft and relatively fresh. The older it is, the more chance there is that any parasites will have died and can't be detected."

A plastic scoop is a simple and mess-free way to pick up stool samples.

Blood in Urine

Even a tiny amount of blood in the urethra or bladder can give urine a pinkish tint. It's scary to see, but most of the time, the underlying problem won't be serious and will clear up quickly with the right treatment. But because veterinarians have identified more than 50 different conditions, some of them quite serious, that can cause blood to appear in the urine, this is one symptom you'll always want to have checked by your vet.

The Usual Suspects

Bladder infection. The lining of the bladder is extremely sensitive, and even minor infections can irritate the tissue and cause a little bit of bleeding, says Anna Scholey, D.V.M., a veterinarian in private practice in Dallas. You should suspect this type of infection when the urine has drops or streaks of bright red blood, she adds. Bladder infections are usually easy to treat because antibiotics concentrate in the urine, making them very effective.

Kidney infection. Unlike the bright red blood in dogs with bladder infections, kidney infections usually make the urine uniformly dark and foul-smelling. The kidneys are responsible for filtering many of the body's wastes, so any infection can be quite serious.

Bladder stones. The urine is filled with minerals that normally stay in solution and pass out of the body along with the fluid. But in dogs who are prone to bladder stones, the minerals periodically clump together, forming hard little

CALL FOR HELP

Because their urinary tracts are shorter than those of males, female dogs have a much higher risk of getting bladder infections. More serious by far are uterine infections. While infections in the reproductive tract aren't very common, they can be life-threatening unless they're treated quickly.

Dogs with uterine infections will usually stay at the veterinarian's overnight, and they'll probably receive intravenous antibiotics. Veterinarians usually recommend spaying them at the same time.

stones. Once a stone forms, more and more minerals cling to it, so the stones increase in size. Bladder stones, also called uroliths, can irritate the lining of the bladder, causing bleeding. If they get large enough, they can block the flow of urine, Dr. Scholey says.

Estrus. Female dogs who are in heat will usually "spot," leaving small blood spots everywhere they go. The blood isn't actually in the urine, but sometimes blood from the vagina will mix with the urine, making it reddish. Smaller breeds usually come into heat twice a year, while larger breeds usually have one heat cycle a year.

Prostate problems. Male dogs with blood in the urine sometimes have prostate infections. Other symptoms of a prostate infection include a swollen penis and testicles.

Poisoning. Many rodent poisons have flavors that dogs like, and they contain chemicals that cause internal bleeding, which may appear in the urine. Other signs of poisoning include vomiting, diarrhea, or restlessness. Dogs who have gotten into rodent poisons will usually be given an injection of vitamin K, which can reverse the effects.

Injuries. Dogs who have taken a hard fall or been hit by a car may look fine, but blood in the urine is a telltale sign that they have suffered internal injuries.

The Best Care

Get help right away. Even though blood in the urine is rarely a sign of serious problems, there's no way to tell at home what's an emergency and what isn't. And since bloody urine may be a sign of internal bleeding, you should consider it an emergency and take your dog to the vet right away, says Dr. Scholey.

Provide plenty of fresh water. The more dogs drink, the more they urinate, and that makes it easier for the body to flush bacteria out of the urinary tract, says Dan Carey, D.V.M., a veterinarian with the Iams pet food company in Dayton, Ohio. In addition, water dilutes the urine, which can help to reduce the irritation that bladder infections cause.

Read food labels. Some dogs never get a urinary tract infection, while others get them all the time. One way to reduce the risk is to give dogs a food that's high in animal proteins, which makes the urine slightly acidic, says Dr. Carey. Bacteria find it difficult to thrive in acidic urine, he explains.

Giving dogs ample chances to urinate will allow them to flush out their bladders and reduce the risk of bladder infections. If you can't be there to let your dog out frequently, consider installing a doggy door so that he can let himself out whenever he needs to.

Stop infections with vitamin C. Many vets have found that giving dogs vitamin C can help treat and prevent bladder infections—both by stimulating the immune system and by making the urine more acidic, says Dr. Scholey. She recommends giving dogs weighing 20 pounds and under up to 250 milligrams a day of vitamin C. Dogs up to 50 pounds can take 500 milligrams a day, and larger dogs can take 750 to 1,000 milligrams a day. It's fine to give dogs vitamin C every day for two weeks or until the symptoms have gone away, Dr. Scholey says.

Take them outside more often. The more frequently dogs urinate, the less opportunity there is for bacteria to accumulate in the bladder, says Dr. Carey. Even though some dogs can last 12 hours or more without a break, this can dramatically increase their risk of getting infections. When you can't take your dog outside yourself, you might want to install a doggy door so that he can let himself out.

41

Breathing Difficulties

Breathing problems are scary because dogs need tremendous amounts of oxygen just to survive. Even a slightly reduced oxygen intake can make them tired and weak. More important, the conditions that cause pets to have trouble breathing can affect other parts of the body as well.

Occasionally, dogs have trouble breathing for obvious reasons—there's something caught in the windpipe, for example. More often, there's an internal problem that's making them struggle to pull in enough oxygen.

Regardless of the cause, dogs who are having trouble breathing will be very uncomfortable and will need all the relief you can provide, says Jerry Woodfield, D.V.M., a veterinary cardiologist in private practice in Seattle.

The Usual Suspects

Anemia. People usually think of anemia as causing fatigue—which it does—but it also makes it hard to breathe, says Rance Sellon, D.V.M., a veterinarian specializing in internal medicine at Washington State University in Pullman. Dogs with anemia don't have enough red blood cells to efficiently carry oxygen through the body, explains Dr. Sellon.

The most common type of anemia is caused by bleeding. Dogs who have been injured or are bleeding internally can quickly become anemic, says Dr. Sellon. Anemia can also be caused by some rodent poisons, which dogs occasionally get into.

In small dogs and puppies, even a heavy infestation of fleas can cause anemia. "Fleas can ingest so many of the red blood cells that dogs develop anemia and shortness of breath," explains Agnes Rupley, D.V.M., a veterinarian in private practice in College Station, Texas.

"Dogs with anemia usually appear weak or tired, and they have pale gums," says Dr. Woodfield. (Some dogs naturally have black or very

---

SUMMER TROUBLE

Panting acts like a canine air conditioner. It removes heat from inside the body and helps dogs keep their temperatures within the normal range of 99.5°F to 102.5°F.

Some panting is normal, but dogs who are breathing rapidly and blowing out a lot of hot air could be developing heatstroke, a dangerous condition in which the body's internal temperature shoots above 104°F.

Heatstroke can cause other symptoms as well, such as drooling, dark red gums, or weakness. It's most common in the warm months, but it can occur any time dogs get too hot. Heatstroke is always an emergency. If you can't get your dog to a vet right away, dunk him in a cold tub, spray him with the hose, or pack ice around his body. Then get him to a veterinarian as quickly as you can.

---

dark gums; you can check for a healthy pink color by looking at the inside of a lower eyelid.)

Dogs with anemia may breathe normally when they're resting, but exertion, stress, or excitement can make it difficult. Dogs with anemia need to be under a veterinarian's care, but it's usually not difficult to restore red blood cells to healthy levels.

Heart disease. The most common reason dogs have trouble breathing is also one of the most serious, says Dr. Woodfield. Dogs with congestive heart failure, a condition in which fluids accumulate in the heart and decrease the amount of blood that's in circulation, will breathe as quickly as they can in order to transport more oxygen through the body.

Heartworms. Carried by mosquitoes, heartworms are parasites that spend their lives in the heart or lungs, blocking blood vessels, damaging tissues, and making breathing difficult, says C. Dave Richards, D.V.M., a veterinarian in private practice in Valdosta, Georgia.

Infections. Whether infections are caused by a flu virus or by bacteria in the respiratory tract, they cause the body to produce mucus and also cause tissues in the nose and throat to swell, making it hard for dogs to breathe, says Dr. Rupley. Infections usually come on quickly and may be accompanied by other symptoms, such as fever, low energy, or a loss of appetite.

Obstructions. It's not uncommon for dogs to literally inhale objects, which may get stuck in their airways. "I've seen chew toys, large pieces of food, rocks, and even tennis balls get stuck in the throat or windpipe," says Taylor Wallace, D.V.M., a veterinarian in private practice in Seattle.

Dogs with short noses, such as Boston terriers, have narrow airways that act almost like

All of the short-faced breeds, such as British bulldogs, have a tendency to develop breathing problems because of their exceptionally short noses.

CALL FOR HELP

Even though some minor problems, such as mild infections, can make it hard for dogs to breathe, more often there's something seriously wrong. Dogs who are gasping, choking, or coughing, or who are so fatigued they're almost falling asleep on their feet need to see a veterinarian right away.

In an emergency situation, your dog may need help breathing. If your dog is lying down, put him on his side. "Keep his neck straight and don't let anything cover his face," says Taylor Wallace, D.V.M., a veterinarian in private practice in Seattle.

natural obstructions, Dr. Wallace adds. "Their anatomy can partially obstruct air flow through the nose and mouth."

Overweight. A common cause of breathing problems—and one of the easiest to fix—is overweight. Dogs who have been visiting the food bowl too often may have extra amounts of fat on their chests and stomachs, and this can make it hard for them to breathe.

The Best Care

Feed them well. Giving dogs a balanced diet will help them recover from many types of anemia, says Craig N. Carter, D.V.M., Ph.D., a veterinarian at Texas A&M University in College Station. Veterinarians sometimes recommend giving dogs a prescription food that is high in minerals, protein, and vitamins. But

don't give dogs iron supplements because they could be toxic, cautions Dr. Carter.

But don't feed them too well. A large percentage of dogs in this country are overweight, which means there's a lot more gasping and panting than there should be. Daily exercise is helpful for losing weight, but giving dogs the proper diet is even more important. Veterinarians recommend giving overweight dogs a low-calorie, high-fiber food, available from veterinarians and in pet supply stores. At the same time, you'll want to put a little less food in the bowl and give treats a little less often.

Dogs who haven't lost weight after a few weeks of reduced eating should be started on a weight-loss plan designed by a veterinarian.

Medications for heartworm come in the form of a chewy treat that dogs don't mind taking, and they are very effective for long-term protection.

Keep them calm. Regardless of what's making dogs struggle to breathe, you don't want to let them get wound up and excited because that causes the body to demand more blood and oxygen—oxygen that may not be available right away. "Try to calm and soothe a dog who's fighting for breath," recommends Dr. Wallace.

Check for obvious problems. It's not always easy to tell whether dogs are having trouble breathing because something is stuck in the windpipe or nostrils. "Look around for any clues that might explain the breathing problem, such as a broken toy," Dr. Wallace says. And take a moment to pry open the mouth and look inside. Even though it's not safe to try to remove most objects at home, at least you'll know whether or not you need to get your dog to a veterinarian, she says.

Take action against heartworms. These dangerous parasites are difficult to get rid of once dogs are infected, but they're easy to prevent with monthly medications. As a bonus, some of the medicines that prevent heartworm will also prevent other worms and parasites.

GIVING ARTIFICIAL RESPIRATION

If a dog stops breathing, you will have to act quickly to get his lungs working again and move oxygen throughout the body.

1 First, put your dog on his side with his neck straight. Open his mouth, and extend his tongue to make sure the airway is open.

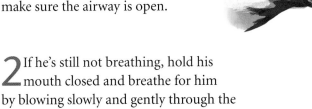

2 If he's still not breathing, hold his mouth closed and breathe for him by blowing slowly and gently through the nose. Keep doing this until he starts breathing on his own, or until you can get him to a veterinarian.

Chewing Objects

Dogs chew as naturally as they jump up at the sight of a leash. They developed the habit in the days when dinner was a no-frills affair—usually a whole carcass that had to be chomped and chewed into manageable chunks. Today's dogs eat haute cuisine by comparison, and their food comes in convenient, bite-size pieces. But the urge to chew is still there. When they're not eating food, they're just as happy eating other things, no matter how inappropriate they may be—such as chair legs, tennis balls, or their owners' new leather loafers.

If it weren't for the fact that dogs occasionally destroy things they shouldn't, chewing is a good habit because it keeps their teeth clean. It's also a great way for dogs to blow off steam and release nervous energy, says Linda Goodloe, Ph.D., a certified applied animal behaviorist with practices in New York City and Philadelphia.

No one would complain about chewing if dogs quit doing it once they were out of their puppy phase, or if all they chewed were their own toys. But some dogs keep chewing all their lives, and it seems like some of them chew everything except their own toys.

The Usual Suspects

Teething. Puppies start chewing at about four months when their puppy teeth are falling out and their adult teeth are coming in. "Their mouths are sore and gnawing relieves the pressure," says Robert J. Garcia, D.V.M., a veterinarian in private practice in San Jose,

BREED SPECIFIC

Dogs bred for hunting and retrieving, such as spaniels and Labrador retrievers, have an instinctive urge to put things in their mouths. However, they've been bred to have "soft" mouths, which means they tend to hold or carry items in their mouths, rather than chomping and destroying them.

California. Puppies have all their adult teeth at about six months, but they usually keep chewing for a while as the teeth settle into the gums.

Exploratory chewing. Once dogs have finished teething, they go through a phase of more strenuous chewing as they use their teeth to explore the world.

Anxiety. Many dogs get lonely or frightened when they're alone and chewing provides a

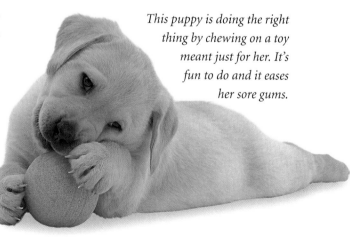

This puppy is doing the right thing by chewing on a toy meant just for her. It's fun to do and it eases her sore gums.

useful distraction, says Dr. Goodloe. Chewing their own toys helps, but chewing their owners' belongings is more appealing because then they're surrounded by human scent, which helps them feel less lonesome, she adds.

Boredom. Dogs were not designed to sleep on the rug all day. They need a lot of exercise and physical and mental activity. When they don't get them, they quickly become bored and start looking for ways to amuse themselves. "Chewing fits the bill perfectly," says Dr. Goodloe. "Anything that's conveniently lying around is fair game for their questing jaws."

It's fun. Chewing isn't always serious business. Dogs enjoy chewing and find it very satisfying to work their jaws and sink their teeth into a variety of objects—if not their toys, then garden hoses, electrical cords, or expensive furniture.

The Best Care

Ease the puppy pain. A puppy's urge to chew is a lot stronger than your desire to make her stop. Apart from keeping your possessions out of your puppy's reach, about all you can do is ease the gum pain so that she has less of a need to chew, says Dr. Garcia. One way to do this is to put one of her chew toys in the freezer for an hour or two, then give it to her to work over. Most puppies like chewing cold things, and the cold acts as a temporary anesthetic and numbs the gums.

Stop them early. Most dogs outgrow their chewing phases by the time they reach adulthood, but some never give it up, usually because their owners put up with it and it becomes a habit, says Dr. Garcia.

This boxer is willing to relinquish things that he shouldn't chew, such as his owner's shoes, when he's offered a tempting chew treat—and then praised for accepting it.

"When you allow a puppy to chew your things, he'll think he has your permission to keep on chewing when he's an adult," he says.

Rather than scolding dogs for chewing the wrong things, it's more effective to give them things they can chew, then reward them when they show an interest, says Lowell Ackerman, D.V.M., Ph.D., a veterinary dermatologist in private practice in Mesa, Arizona. Every dog has different preferences, however, so you'll have to expect some trial and error while searching for acceptable chew toys that dogs like better than your sneakers.

Keep them occupied. Dogs who are anxious or bored—a group that includes nearly every dog who isn't physically or mentally active—are desperate for entertainment. Apart from taking them for more walks, an excellent solution is to give them more exciting toys. Brands such as Kongs and Buster Cubes are good choices because they're made of hard materials that give a satisfying level of resistance to canine jaws. They can also be loaded with food, which gives dogs a mental challenge as they'll put in a lot of effort to get to the goodies inside. As a bonus, the hidden food rewards them for chewing their own toys, making them less likely to return to your things.

Like children, it doesn't take dogs long to get bored with toys, however. Rather than buying them one or two chew toys, buy a half-dozen. But don't put them out all at once. Each day, put one toy away and bring another one out. That way, they'll always think they're getting something new, says Dr. Goodloe.

Try some sabotage. While some dogs chew anything and everything, others develop a powerful urge for one particular thing. They may start chewing it because its size and texture are appealing, and then keep returning to it because they're attracted by the personal smell they've left behind. By coating the object with Bitter Apple pet repellent or even a bit of chili sauce, the fixation for the object will soon start to fade. Start by coating an inconspicuous place to make sure the object won't stain.

Dogs hate surprises, which is why some experts recommend booby-trapping their chews of choice by putting a few coins in an empty can and running a string from the can to the object you're trying to protect. The can will come clattering down, and the noise may shock dogs into better behavior.

CHEW TOYS

There are literally hundreds of chew toys, but the ones dogs are attracted to the most are those made from natural substances, such as rawhides, bones, and pigs' ears. Natural chews taste a little bit like animals, which dogs adore. They're often meaty and salty, and they have a size and texture that allows the jaws to get a very good workout.

The drawback to natural chews is that they usually don't last very long. Many people find that it's more economical to buy rubber, nylon, or plastic toys. Many dogs are perfectly happy with these, too, especially when they're coated (or filled) with a little bit of food.

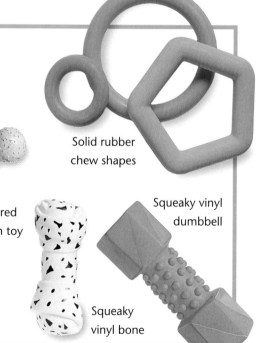

Solid rubber chew shapes

Mint-flavored fresh breath toy

Squeaky vinyl dumbbell

Squeaky vinyl bone

Choking

There's a structure called the pharynx at the entrance to the throat at the back of the mouth. The pharynx routes air into the trachea, the tube that leads to the lungs, and food into the esophagus, the tube that leads to the stomach. When air goes the wrong way, it doesn't matter much. But when food or other foreign objects go in the wrong direction, dogs will erupt with gags and hacks.

Gagging and gasping don't always mean that a dog is choking, says Karen Zagorsky, D.V.M., a veterinarian in private practice in Moreno Valley, California. Dogs often retch and regurgitate for a few seconds. "By contrast, a dog who's really choking can't catch his breath and is in great distress," she says.

The Usual Suspects

Food. If dogs ate in restaurants, every waiter would have to be trained in first-aid. Dogs usually take their food in great, gulping mouthfuls, a throwback to their days in the wild when dogs who ate the fastest thrived, while those who held back tended to go hungry. Dogs eat so greedily, in fact, that they often swallow more food than they can handle, which frequently causes choking. Dogs who are choking can't get a good breath and will lose consciousness quickly if someone isn't nearby to help them out.

Swallowed objects. Golf balls and even tennis balls are common causes of choking. Nearly all dogs love balls and will grab them with so much enthusiasm that the balls go farther back in the throat than they should, says Kenneth Lyon, D.V.M., a veterinary dental specialist in private practice in Mesa, Arizona.

The Best Care

Ease it out. A choking dog needs emergency care, and unless the choking happens in the veterinarian's office, it's up to you to remove whatever it is that's causing the problem. "If you can see the object and remove it easily, go for it," says John Daugherty, D.V.M., a veterinarian in private practice in Poland, Ohio.

A choking dog is a panicking dog, however, and you might get bitten when you reach into the mouth. If possible, put on some heavy gloves when reaching inside. If you don't have gloves, you may have no choice but to wait for a few seconds. Once a dog's oxygen levels decline, fainting occurs fairly quickly, and at that point, you'll be able to reach in with much less risk, says Dr. Daugherty.

Get help quickly. Any object that's stuck deeply enough in the throat to cause choking may be difficult to remove at home. Don't waste too much time unless you think that you have a good chance of getting it out. You may be better off getting your dog to the veterinarian right away. "Many dogs who have things stuck in their throats can still breathe well enough, provided you can keep them calm, to be transported to a veterinarian's, where they can receive professional treatment," says Suann Hosie, D.V.M., a veterinarian in private practice at

49

an emergency clinic in Vancouver, British Columbia, Canada.

Do the Heimlich maneuver. This is a very efficient technique for removing objects causing choking, and it doesn't take special skills to do it. "Heimlich maneuvers sometimes save the day," says Lynn Harpold, D.V.M., a veterinarian in private practice in Mesa, Arizona.

THE HEIMLICH MANEUVER

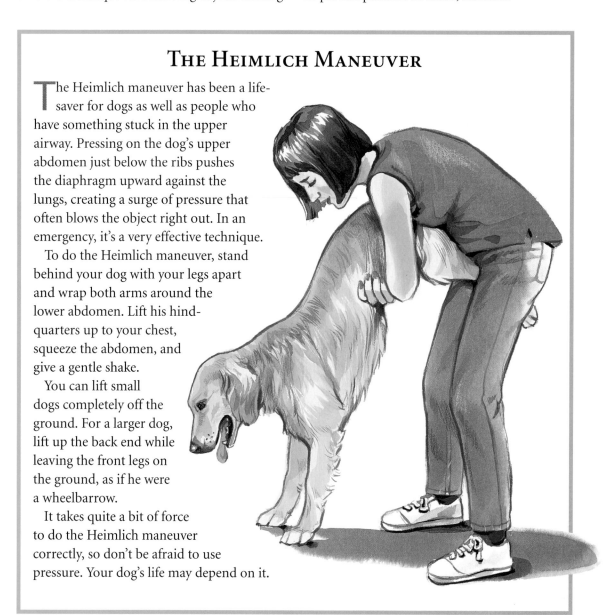

The Heimlich maneuver has been a lifesaver for dogs as well as people who have something stuck in the upper airway. Pressing on the dog's upper abdomen just below the ribs pushes the diaphragm upward against the lungs, creating a surge of pressure that often blows the object right out. In an emergency, it's a very effective technique.

To do the Heimlich maneuver, stand behind your dog with your legs apart and wrap both arms around the lower abdomen. Lift his hindquarters up to your chest, squeeze the abdomen, and give a gentle shake.

You can lift small dogs completely off the ground. For a larger dog, lift up the back end while leaving the front legs on the ground, as if he were a wheelbarrow.

It takes quite a bit of force to do the Heimlich maneuver correctly, so don't be afraid to use pressure. Your dog's life may depend on it.

Coat Changes

The hairs in a dog's coat consist of a tough, fibrous protein called keratin, which is protected and lubricated by oils produced in tiny glands in the skin. Not every dog's coat has the same degree of sheen. Some breeds have hair that's naturally coarser or more oily than others. But in general, the coat should be glossy and odor-free. A change in the coat's usual appearance—when it turns dull, dry, greasy, matted, or smelly—means that something's out of balance somewhere in the body.

The Usual Suspects

Problems with the diet. Dogs who develop dull, dry coats may not be getting enough of a substance called cis-linoleic acid in their diets, says Lowell Ackerman, D.V.M., Ph.D, a veterinary dermatologist in private practice in Mesa, Arizona. Most commercial dog foods provide plenty of this substance, although some of it may be lost when kibble is stored for too long.

Seborrhea. It takes about three weeks for skin cells to mature, travel from the inner layer of skin to the surface, and die and flake off. In dogs with a condition called seborrhea, however, this process is accelerated. Dead cells quickly accumulate, making the skin and coat look dry and flaky. The combination of oils and skin "debris" provides a fertile breeding ground for bacteria, so dogs with seborrhea often get skin infections, making them itchy and smelly. The coat will be greasy, and there may be oily, brownish scales on the elbows, hocks, and ears.

Too many baths. Dogs don't need baths anywhere near as often as humans. Washing dogs too often strips natural oils from the coat, making it look dry and dull.

Age. The entire body slows down as dogs get older. Oils and nutrients take longer to reach the skin, which is why older dogs often have coats that are somewhat dry and tired-looking.

Lack of brushing. Regular grooming does more than make dogs look good. It removes hairs as they're shed, preventing them from accumulating next to the skin. In dogs who aren't brushed, this hair essentially forms a thick blanket that prevents air from reaching the skin and reduces the efficiency of the oil glands. It also makes the surface of the skin hot and humid, leading to hot spots and other skin infections.

The Best Care

Put more oil in their diets. Adding cis-linoleic acid to your dog's diet is often the best way to put more sheen in the coat, says Dr. Ackerman. Oils that contain cis-linoleic acid include safflower, sunflower, and flaxseed oils. Try

BREED SPECIFIC

Seborrhea is thought to be a hereditary problem, and American cocker spaniels, English springer spaniels, and West Highland white terriers have a high risk of getting it.

mixing one of these oils into your dog's food every day, Dr. Ackerman says. For small dogs, add about a teaspoon of oil. Medium-size dogs can have two teaspoons, and large dogs can have a tablespoon. It takes time for oil in the diet to reach the coat so you probably won't see results for a month or two, he explains.

Use a medicated shampoo. Even though most dogs don't need frequent baths, dogs with seborrhea will usually improve when they're washed once a week with a medicated shampoo. Veterinarians usually recommend using an oil-dissolving shampoo that contains sulfur or coal tar. Work up a lather and let it stand for about 10 minutes, advises Lila Miller, D.V.M., senior director of animal sciences and veterinary adviser of the American Society for the Prevention of Cruelty to Animals in New York City. Then rinse your dog very thoroughly.

Brush often. Brushing dogs helps to remove hair and improve air circulation around the skin and through the coat. In addition, it stimulates glands to produce more oil, which helps give coats their pleasing sheen, says Michael T. Cavanaugh, D.V.M., a veterinarian in private practice in Fort Collins, Colorado.

Brushing is most effective when you use firm, short, deep strokes. Begin by brushing from head to tail. Then make a second pass going from tail to head. Brushing against the direction of hair growth helps dislodge dead hairs. The coat will usually start looking better within two weeks of daily brushings. After that, you can do it less often—once every few days or once a week is usually plenty.

While regular brushing is always good, some breeds, such as pointers, Labrador retrievers, and Chesapeake Bay retrievers, don't need as much attention. Their coats are naturally oily. In fact, they act like a slightly oily mackintosh and have water-resistant properties. Too much brushing will reduce the effectiveness of the waterproof coating.

Bathe only when you have to. Dogs' coats are naturally self-cleaning, and there's no reason to bathe them frequently unless they're unusually dirty. Outdoor dogs generally need a bath once a month, while most indoor dogs can get by with yearly baths. Vets recommend using shampoos that are made for dogs because many human shampoos are too harsh and will strip off the protective oils. Baby shampoo works well, however. So does a mild dishwashing liquid.

FAST FIX A quick way to put shine in a dog's coat is to rub it well with a mixture of cornstarch and talcum powder, or with dry oat bran that's been slightly warmed. Then brush out the coat. The bran or cornstarch will soak up grime and oil.

Warmed oat bran or cornstarch mixed with talcum powder makes an effective dry shampoo.

Confusion

There are few things more unsettling than watching dogs who have lost some of their mental bearings. Their heads cock, their ears pull back, and their eyes look blank and glazed. You can see the confusion, and it's a frightening sight.

"Just as with people, when dogs age, there is some degeneration of the nerves," says Joe Butterweck, D.V.M., a veterinarian in private practice in Fresno, California. Older dogs may also lose some of their sight or hearing, which adds to their physical and emotional confusion.

Confusion is never normal, however, Dr. Butterweck adds. Whether your dog is in his senior years or the prime of life, confusion usually means that there's a physical problem that needs looking into.

The Usual Suspects

Head injuries. Dogs have thinner skulls than people, and even mild jolts or bumps to

CALL FOR HELP

Mental confusion is a serious symptom and should always be a signal to take your dog to the veterinarian. Even if your pet is elderly, don't assume that the problem is simply old age. Old dogs and cats shouldn't be confused by their surroundings. If they are, there is clearly something wrong.

BREED SPECIFIC

Short-nosed breeds such as pugs (below), Pekingese, and bulldogs are more likely than other breeds to get heatstroke because they have short air passages, which limit their ability to dispel body heat by panting.

the head can make them dazed and disoriented. The confusion is usually temporary, however, and most dogs will recover fairly quickly.

Seizures. We think of epileptic seizures as causing dramatic symptoms, such as thrashing or gnashing of the teeth. But many dogs with epilepsy have very mild symptoms—a few minutes or hours of confusion, for example, or a little bit of shaking. Dogs with epilepsy always need to be under a veterinarian's care, but in most cases, the seizures themselves are harmless.

Pressure on the brain. Anything that presses on the brain, whether it's a tumor or swelling caused by an infection, can cause dogs to become disoriented, says John Saidla, D.V.M., director of continuing education at the College of Veterinary Medicine at Cornell University in Ithaca, New York.

Distemper. "If a dog contracts distemper or has a very high fever at a young age, he may act

Giving dogs access to cool, shady resting spots can help prevent heatstroke, a common cause of confusion.

Heatstroke. Dogs don't perspire very much, and the only way they dispel heat is by panting. When they can't pant enough to cool off, they may develop heatstroke, which can lead to confusion and extreme exhaustion.

The Best Care

Make life predictable. Regardless of what's causing confusion, you'll want to do everything you can to keep your dog comfortable, safe, and reassured, says Dr. Johnson. This is especially true for older pets who have become somewhat senile. Confused pets are often frightened pets,

confused later on," says Susanne B. Johnson, Ph.D., an animal behaviorist in private practice in Beaverdam, Virginia.

Diabetes. Dogs with diabetes have high levels of sugar in the blood, but very little of this sugar is able to get into the brain. Without adequate supplies of sugar, they may get disoriented and confused, says Dr. Saidla.

If it turns out that your pet has low blood sugar, there are a number of medications, including insulin, that will help restore it to healthy levels. In addition, your veterinarian may recommend putting your pet on a custom-designed diet and exercise plan, which also will help keep blood sugar in balance.

Poisons. Poisoning is a very common cause of mental confusion, mainly because there are so many household chemicals that dogs get into, ranging from cleaners in kitchen cupboards to antifreeze in the garage. Other symptoms of poisoning include vomiting, dizziness, or difficulty walking or standing up.

As they get older, many pets will experience a degree of confusion. Giving them extra time and attention will help them stay calm.

and giving them extra attention will help them stay calm and relaxed.

You'll also want to minimize changes to their surroundings. Knowing where everything is—including their food and water bowls—will help them feel more secure. "Don't expect your senior to perform at his top level," adds Dr. Johnson. "Avoid surprises and keep to the same routine as much as you can."

Avoid seizure triggers. Seizures themselves usually aren't dangerous, but they can leave dogs frightened and confused. Dogs with epilepsy tend to have seizures when they are over-stimulated, so veterinarians recommend keeping them calm—by reducing their exposure to loud noises, for example, and keeping the activities around them low-key.

Stabilize blood sugar. Veterinarians have found that even dogs who need insulin to control diabetes usually maintain better blood sugar levels when they eat several small meals a day instead of one or two large meals. Eating frequent meals helps keep blood sugar levels steady, as opposed to the ups and downs that occur when dogs eat only once a day. In addition, your veterinarian may recommend putting your dog on a prescription diet, which will also help keep blood sugar steady.

Keep them cool. Heatstroke is among the most dangerous conditions that dogs can get, sometimes leading to brain damage in just a few hours. The best protection is to make sure dogs always have shade to retire to when they're spending time outside, and to watch them carefully when you're walking or playing in hot weather. Dogs who are at the point of developing heatstroke will pant heavily, and their

Some viruses can lead to brain infections that cause confusion. While these viruses can be serious, they're also easily prevented by regular vaccinations.

tongues may be bright red. They'll also be on the point of collapsing from exhaustion.

If you even suspect that your dog has heatstroke, you need to get him to a veterinarian right away, says Dr. Butterweck. If for some reason that's not possible, do everything you can to lower your dog's temperature—by putting him in a bathtub filled with cool water, for example, or by spraying him with the hose. Then get him to the vet as soon as you can.

Vaccinate regularly. Viruses such as distemper can cause encephalitis, a brain infection that can cause extreme confusion—and worse. Keeping your dog's vaccinations up-to-date is the only way to prevent canine distemper. Your vet will give the shots, but it's up to you to get your pet to the vet when they are due. It's worth doing because there isn't a cure for distemper. A few minutes of prevention now will help ensure that he stays sharp, alert, and healthy later on.

Constipation

As anyone who owns a Pooper Scooper can attest, most dogs don't have a problem with constipation. Their digestive tracts are supremely efficient, which is nature's way of coping with their voracious—and often inappropriate—appetites. But sometimes their stools are either too hard or too small to stimulate the wavelike intestinal movements that help the body to get rid of them. Or maybe the intestines have lost some of their "push." Either way, the result is a lack of regularity.

It's not always easy to tell when dogs are constipated because every dog has different bowel habits. Some dogs have three or more bowel movements a day, while others have just one. The only reliable guideline is to know your dog's usual pattern, says Dan Carey, D.V.M., a veterinarian with the Iams pet food company in Dayton, Ohio. There's no need to rush into action when dogs get constipated, Dr. Carey adds. Stools that accumulate for a day or two won't do any harm and will usually pass on their own fairly quickly. Constipation that lasts more than two days, however, or that causes serious pain or straining needs to be taken care of.

The Usual Suspects

Too little fiber. Dietary fiber, the indigestible, healthful stuff found in vegetables, cereals, and legumes, has been called nature's scrub brush because it helps stools move more quickly through the body. Most commercial dog foods contain a lot of cereals which are very high in fiber. Dogs who mainly eat meat, however, may not be getting enough fiber to stay regular.

Not enough water. The stools absorb large amounts of water in the digestive tract, and as they swell, they stimulate the intestines. Dogs who don't drink much water—because it's not available or because their thirst mechanisms aren't as sensitive as they should be—often get constipated because the stools are too hard and small to stimulate intestinal movements.

Lack of exercise. The large intestine is a muscle, and like any muscle it needs regular exercise to work efficiently. "If your dog just lies around, so does his digestive tract," says Bill Martin, D.V.M., a veterinarian in private practice in Fletcher, North Carolina.

This Dalmatian is having a great time chewing on plastic, but the broken pieces that are sure to accumulate could block the intestine.

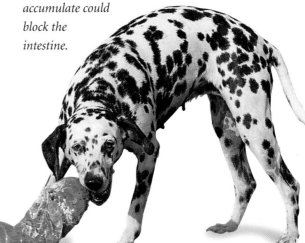

Exercising often and vigorously is what keeps these golden retrievers happy—and regular.

Overweight. Dogs who are a little pudgy are more likely to get constipated because fat deposits in the abdomen can interfere with the intestines' normal movements. Overweight dogs also tend to get less exercise, and this makes the intestines work less efficiently, says Dr. Martin.

Eating trash. Dogs who snack on garbage are more likely to get diarrhea than constipation, except when they eat cardboard, paper, or plastic, which can partially block the digestive tract and make it harder for stools to get through.

The Best Care

Give them additional fiber. Most dogs get plenty of dietary fiber in their regular food, but you can give a little extra to relieve temporary bouts of constipation. One of the best sources of supplemental fiber is psyllium, says Anna Scholey, D.V.M., a veterinarian in private practice in Dallas. You can buy psyllium husks in bulk form, or you can get psyllium capsules in health food stores. Metamucil, an over-the-counter laxative, contains a lot of psyllium and is entirely safe for dogs, Dr. Scholey adds. You can give dogs one to three capsules of psyllium a day, depending on their size. If you're using Metamucil, sprinkle or mix it into the food—use about a half-teaspoon a day for small dogs and up to two teaspoons a day for larger dogs. Unprocessed oat bran is another great way of increasing fiber intake, adds Dr. Scholey. Buy it from supermarkets or health food stores and mix with their usual food. Give one teaspoon per day for small dogs, two teaspoons for medium dogs, and three teaspoons for large dogs.

An easier way to get more fiber in your dog's diet is to mix cooked, whole-grain pasta or lightly steamed vegetables such as broccoli or carrots in his food, says Dr. Scholey. Fiber works fairly quickly, and most dogs will have a bowel movement within a day after getting the extra amounts.

While some fiber helps the digestive tract work more smoothly, giving too much can slow it down, especially if your dog isn't drinking enough water, says Dr. Carey. "People sometimes give their dogs extra fiber in the form of psyllium husks or wheat bran," he explains. "This can increase the volume of the stools, but it also decreases their moisture."

It's fine to give dogs extra fiber as long as they're also drinking extra water, he adds. One way to encourage dogs to drink more is to add some flavor to their regular water—by adding a bouillon cube, for example, or even by giving them a sports drink such as Gatorade. Many dogs like the taste and will gladly drink extra.

Exercise the insides. Dogs who get plenty of exercise are much less likely to get constipated than those who lie around all day, says Dr. Carey. Any exercise is good, but it's most effective 15 to 20 minutes after dogs have eaten, when the urge to have a bowel movement is strongest. Dogs need at least 20 to 30 minutes of exercise twice a day, adds Dr. Carey.

The one exception to after-dinner exercise is when you have a large, deep-chested dog, such as a boxer or Great Dane. These dogs have a high risk of bloat, a dangerous condition in which air gets trapped in the stomach. You can reduce the risk by giving them an hour of quiet time before and after eating, says Dr. Scholey.

Feed them more often. "The stomach and colon have this agreement: When the stomach takes in food, it notifies the colon to get ready," says Dr. Carey. For dogs that tend to get constipated on just one large meal a day, try to stimulate this reflex by feeding them three small meals instead, he says. This may make them more regular.

Giving dogs extra fiber—such as Metamucil or cooked whole-grain pasta and steamed vegetables—will help relieve occasional bouts of constipation.

CALL FOR HELP

If there's one thing that dogs love better than burying bones, it's chewing them. Dogs can reduce the toughest bone to splinters and chips, but these bone fragments sometimes stick to the intestinal lining, making it difficult for stools to pass through. The longer stools stay in place, the harder and larger they get, until they block the passage entirely, says Bill Martin, D.V.M., a veterinarian in private practice in Fletcher, North Carolina. Dogs with this type of constipation, called obstipation, will strain repeatedly to move their bowels and will generally look very uncomfortable. Obstipation can be serious, so it's important to call your vet if your dog isn't able to have a bowel movement for more than a couple of days.

FAST FIX It's no one's idea of fun, but the quickest way to relieve constipation is to give dogs the same type of over-the-counter glycerine suppository that humans use, says Dr. Carey. Lubricate the suppository with a little petroleum jelly or K-Y Jelly and insert it gently into the rectum. It will melt within 5 to 10 minutes, lubricating and softening the stool. After 10 minutes, take your dog outside and wait for nature to take over. For dogs that weigh 20 pounds or less, give the pediatric size once a day. Larger dogs can be given adult-size suppositories. If your dog is still constipated after a couple of days, call your veterinarian, Dr. Carey advises.

Coughing

Dogs don't cough anywhere near as often as people, and when they do they probably have a viral infection or some type of bronchitis, says Tim Banker, D.V.M., a veterinarian in private practice in Greensboro, North Carolina. Coughs—and whatever it is that's causing them—will often clear up on their own within a few days. Dogs who keep coughing, however, or who have other symptoms such as fatigue or a loss of appetite, need to see a vet.

The Usual Suspects

Infections. Dogs who have high-pitched, hacking coughs usually have kennel cough. Caused by a variety of viral, bacterial, or fungal infections, kennel cough is rarely serious, but it's highly contagious, says Rolan Tripp, D.V.M., a veterinarian in private practice in La Mirada, California. Despite the name, dogs in kennels rarely get kennel cough these days because owners of boarding kennels usually require that dogs be vaccinated before checking in. As with a cold, flu, or any other infection, dogs can pick up kennel cough just about anywhere, says Dr. Tripp. The infections that cause kennel cough usually clear up within a week or two without any treatment, but the coughs can linger for several weeks. In puppies, or in dogs with other illnesses, kennel cough occasionally turns into a separate, more serious infection that requires veterinary care, says Dr. Banker.

Bronchitis. The lungs contain many narrow airways called bronchi. When the bronchi get irritated—by such things as chemical fumes, cigarette smoke, household sprays, plant pollens, such as ragweed or bluegrass, or other allergens—they become inflamed and narrower, a condition called bronchitis. Dogs with bronchitis often develop a wheezy cough and have difficulty breathing, says Dr. Banker.

The Best Care

Stop the cough. Even though most coughs clear up on their own, the relentless hacking can irritate the throat and make dogs feel tired and sore. Over-the-counter cough syrups will often

The pollens of bluegrass (left) and ragweed (right) often cause allergies—and an uncomfortable, wheezing cough— when they get into a dog's air passages.

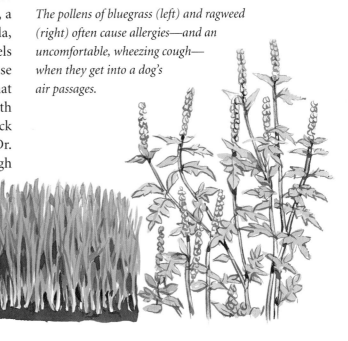

stop coughing fairly quickly, says Anna Scholey, D.V.M., a veterinarian in private practice in Dallas. She recommends using a cough syrup containing the active ingredient dextromethorphan, such as Robitussin maximum strength cough syrup. Dextromethorphan is chemically similar to morphine and acts directly on the brain to suppress the coughing reflex, explains Dr. Scholey. The coating action of the syrup may also help soothe the throat. When the cough is troublesome, give a half-teaspoon to dogs who weigh up to 10 pounds, one teaspoon to dogs around 20 pounds, and two teaspoons to dogs 40 pounds or more.

Stimulate the immune system. Experts have found that giving dogs vitamin C will stimulate the immune system, making it better able to fight off infections, says Dr. Scholey. She recommends giving 100 milligrams of vitamin C a day to small dogs. Medium-size dogs can take 250 milligrams a day, and larger dogs can take 500 milligrams twice a day.

The one problem with vitamin C is that in large amounts it may cause diarrhea, she adds. If your dog develops loose stools, give him about half the usual dose and see if things improve, she advises.

Encourage them to eat. Dogs with kennel cough are often reluctant to eat because their throats are sore, which can be a problem because they need extra nutrients to help their immune systems stave off secondary infections, explains Dr. Banker. One way to encourage dogs to eat is to warm up their food a little, which releases aromas that

stimulate their appetites, says Dr Banker. He also recommends stirring chicken or beef broth into their food. This makes it more appetizing and also softens it so they'll find it a bit easier to get down.

Keep them comfortable and calm. The body has limited resources, and dogs with kennel cough need to conserve their energy to speed the healing process. Dr. Banker recommends giving them a minimum of exercise until they're feeling better. It's also important to keep them warm and dry because exposure to moisture or cold air increases the risk that kennel cough will turn into something more serious, such as pneumonia.

Keep the air clean. Even when bronchitis isn't caused by airborne irritants, breathing pollen, dust, or even perfume invariably makes the irritation worse. Cleaning and dusting more often than usual will help reduce the amount of irritating particles that enter your dog's lungs, says Dr. Banker. Changing air conditioner filters

BREED SPECIFIC

Pekingese (left), bulldogs, and other pug-nosed breeds have a high risk of developing respiratory infections because they have unusually narrow airways inside their relatively flat heads. Not only do they get respiratory infections more often than other dogs, but the infections they do get tend to be more serious.

CALL FOR HELP

The occasional cough is nothing to worry about, but dogs who suddenly start coughing a lot, especially at night or after exercise, need to see a veterinarian right away because this is one of the main signs of congestive heart failure.

In dogs with congestive heart failure, the heart can't pump blood fast enough. This allows fluids to build up in the lungs, causing a persistent cough, says Lowell Ackerman, D.V.M., Ph.D., a veterinary dermatologist in private practice in Mesa, Arizona. Dogs with congestive heart failure usually need medications to help remove the excess fluids from the body. They also may need changes in their diet, such as a switch to a low-salt food, explains Dr. Ackerman.

One cause of congestive heart failure is heartworms, says Dr. Ackerman. Transmitted by mosquitoes, the heartworms can grow up to a foot long and eventually take up residence in the heart and lungs, making them work less efficiently, he adds.

tional collar-and-leash can result in bouts of coughing. A good alternative to a collar is a harness or a head halter, both of which allow you to control your dog without putting pressure on his tender throat.

While harnesses are effective, Dr. Tripp prefers using the head halter, available in pet supply stores. "A harness gives the owner very little control over a dog, whereas a halter won't irritate a dog's throat, while maintaining excellent control," he says.

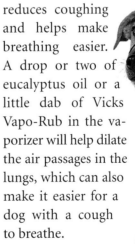 **FAST FIX** One reason dogs cough when they're sick is that infections remove moisture from the delicate tissues in the throat. Humidifying the air with a vaporizer will quickly help replace the moisture that illnesses take out, says Dr. Scholey. Inhaling moist air reduces coughing and helps make breathing easier. A drop or two of eucalyptus oil or a little dab of Vicks Vapo-Rub in the vaporizer will help dilate the air passages in the lungs, which can also make it easier for a dog with a cough to breathe.

A head halter gives great control without irritating the sensitive tissues that line the throat.

about once a month will help. So will using an air-cleaning system called an ozonator. "They help reduce the amount of dust and pollen in the air," he says.

Invest in a head halter. Even dogs who spend most of the day snoozing while recuperating from a cough need to go out for walks now and then. When they have bronchitis, however, even the slight pressure exerted by the tradi-

Dandruff

It isn't painful and it can go on forever without causing problems, which is why people tend to ignore dandruff when it shows up on their dogs. That's a mistake because dandruff is a valuable clue that something's out of balance in the body.

The Usual Suspects

Dry skin. Most dogs with dandruff have skin that's drier than it should be and the skin cells are flaking off quickly enough to be visible on the coat, says Peter S. Sakas, D.V.M., a veterinarian in private practice in Niles, Illinois. Some dogs only get dry skin in the winter, and their dandruff goes away in the moister months of spring and summer. Other dogs have a condition called dry seborrhea, which means they have dry skin because that's the way nature made them.

Even though dandruff doesn't cause symptoms, dry skin does. It can make dogs extremely itchy, says Robert Rizzitano, D.V.M., a veterinarian in private practice in Los Angeles.

Dietary problems. The nutrients in foods supply the organs, muscles, blood, and other parts of the body. The skin, however, is last in the chain of delivery—and the first place where dietary problems show up, says Dan Carey, D.V.M., a veterinarian with the Iams pet food company in Dayton, Ohio.

Dogs need certain nutrients, especially fatty acids, to keep their skin healthy. Most pet foods contain plenty of fatty acids, but some dogs need more than the usual amounts. In addition, dogs who eat homemade diets or generic pet foods may not be getting enough fatty acids, skin-healthy B vitamins, or minerals such as zinc, says Dr. Carey.

Infrequent baths or limited grooming. Dogs don't need baths as much as people do. When they have long hair or thick undercoats, however, fresh air doesn't always reach the skin, allowing dandruff to accumulate. In addition, oil-producing glands in the skin don't always release their cargo evenly. Dogs who aren't bathed or groomed very often may have dry patches on the skin where dandruff accumulates.

Thyroid problems. It doesn't happen often, but dandruff sometimes means that the thyroid

A daily brushing distributes the natural oils through this Border collie's coat, keeping it healthy and dandruff-free.

Drinking More Than Usual

Besides quenching thirst, water regulates body temperature, aids in digestion, and lubricates the tissues. It's almost impossible to overindulge. But the desire to drink tells another story. Dogs who are suddenly drinking excessive amounts of water, a condition called polydipsia, are doing it for a reason. Vets have identified more than 60 conditions, some of them potentially serious, that make dogs drink a lot.

The Usual Suspects

Kidney disease. "When the kidneys can't regulate the body's water content, pets can't retain fluids, so they drink more and urinate it all out," says Craig N. Carter, D.V.M., Ph.D., head of epidemiology at the Texas Veterinary Medical Diagnostic Laboratory at Texas A&M University in College Station.

Diabetes. Diabetes occurs when the pancreas either doesn't produce enough insulin or the insulin it does produce doesn't work as well as it should. Without efficient insulin, sugar levels rise in the bloodstream, and dogs will drink a lot of water in an attempt to maintain the body's normal sugar-to-water balance.

Hot weather. Dogs who spend a lot of time outdoors in hot weather can dehydrate rapidly, and they will often consume huge amounts of water to maintain a normal body temperature.

CHECKING THE BODY'S WATER BALANCE

You'd think that dogs who are drinking huge amounts of water would get waterlogged, but the opposite is true: They often get dehydrated because of an underlying medical problem that's taking water from the body despite their best efforts to keep up.

To check for dehydration, lift the skin on the dog's back near the neck. Release it and see how quickly it snaps back—it should be firm and springy within seconds. When dogs are dehydrated, the skin will creep back slowly or not all. This means their body is very low on water and they need to see a vet right away, says Craig N. Carter, D.V.M., Ph.D., head of epidemiology at the Texas Veterinary Medical Diagnostic Laboratories at Texas A&M University in College Station.

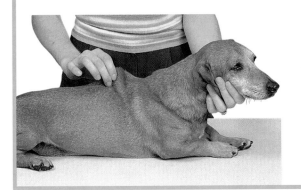

Stress. Veterinarians aren't sure why they do it, but dogs who are feeling anxious and unhappy about something will often drink lots of water. It's possible that the act of drinking distracts them from the goings-on and makes them feel a little calmer. And the more you worry about them, the more they'll drink, adds Karen Overall, V.M.D., Ph.D., head of the behavior clinic at the University of Pennsylvania School of Veterinary Medicine in Philadelphia. "They like the attention," she explains.

Hormone problems. The hormones are responsible for maintaining the body's normal balance of fluids, chemicals, and nutrients—a condition of equilibrium called homeostasis. When the hormones are disrupted by conditions such as Cushing's disease or hyperthyroidism, dogs may drink enormous amounts of water—a gallon or more a day, in some cases—to compensate.

The Best Care

Check the water consumption. Since dogs don't drink from neat little glasses, it's almost impossible to tell whether they're really drinking more than usual or if the amount is excessive. "Measure the amount of water for a few days," suggests Dean Gebroe, D.V.M., a veterinarian in private practice in Los Angeles. Use a measuring cup to fill the bowl. After 24 hours, measure the remaining water. "Call your vet and ask if that's too much," says Dr. Gebroe.

Consider a change of diet. Veterinarians have found that a few simple changes in diet will often help dogs who have diabetes. The easiest change is to give them several small meals a day instead of one big one. This allows sugars to enter the bloodstream gradually rather than all at once, preventing blood sugar "spikes." Losing weight can also be helpful. In fact, dogs with diabetes who lose weight and keep it off sometimes need less insulin. In some cases, they're able to quit taking insulin entirely.

Diabetes is a difficult condition to manage, however, so don't make any changes in diet or medication without checking with your veterinarian first, says Dr. Carter.

FAST FIX It's fine that dogs drink a lot in hot weather—unless you happen to leave for work in the morning and forget to fill the water bowl. If your dog spends a lot of time outside, you may want to get a small wading pool, says Anna Scholey, D.V.M., a veterinarian in private practice in Dallas. That way they get plenty to drink, and many dogs are only too happy to climb in now and then to cool off.

A child's wading pool filled with water provides an extra-large drinking bowl as well as a source of entertainment on a hot day.

Drooling

Veterinarians hear a lot of complaints about drooling, and most of the time their advice is pretty simple: Live with it. Nearly all dogs drool when they're excited or waiting for breakfast, and some dogs drool almost all the time. Apart from tying a bandanna around their necks to catch the moisture, there isn't much you can do about it.

It's not this simple when there's been a recent change in your dog's drooling habits. Dogs who are suddenly drooling more than usual invariably have a problem, says Karen Zagorsky, D.V.M., a veterinarian in private practice in Moreno Valley, California.

The Usual Suspects

Bloat. A dangerous condition that usually occurs in large, deep-chested dogs, bloat happens when the stomach suddenly fills with air and expands, possibly pressing against major blood vessels in the abdomen.

You should suspect bloat if your dog is drooling after she's eaten, and her stomach is swollen and unusually taut. Dogs with bloat can die in hours, so it's essential to get them to a vet right away. You can't treat bloat at home, but it can often be prevented by giving dogs several small meals a day rather than one big meal. It's also a good idea not to give dogs a lot of food or water for an hour before or after vigorous exercise.

Objects in the mouth. It's not a coincidence that people start salivating the minute a dentist starts working. Anything that goes in the mouth, from a piece of fruit to the end of a pencil, sets off the salivary glands. The same thing happens in dogs. They'll often start drooling when something—often a bit of stick or bone—gets stuck somewhere in the mouth, says John Daugherty, D.V.M., a veterinarian in private practice in Poland, Ohio.

Dental problems. Dogs don't get cavities very often, but more than 80 percent of dogs do get periodontal disease, a condition in which bacteria in the mouth cause irritation or infection in the gums, which in turn results in drooling, says Kenneth Lyon, D.V.M., a veterinary dental specialist in private practice in Mesa, Arizona. Other symptoms of periodontal disease include bad breath, and, in some cases, a reluctance to chew, says Dr. Lyon. Dogs who have broken a tooth also may drool a lot, he adds.

Nausea. It's common for dogs to drool when their stomachs are upset. After a trip in the car, for example, you may discover wet spots on the upholstery. Dogs who are nauseated will often be restless, and they'll pant a lot as well.

Poisoning. Dogs are attracted to all sorts of odd things, including household poisons such as antifreeze and some cleaning fluids. Heavy drooling may be the first sign that

A dishcloth makes an effective bandanna for dogs who tend to drool.

CALL FOR HELP

Now that rabies vaccinations are required by law, it's rare for this terrible disease to occur in dogs—but when it does, heavy drooling is one of the first signs, says Kenneth Lyon, D.V.M., a veterinary dental specialist in private practice in Mesa, Arizona. Rabies is often transmitted by skunks and raccoons, so dogs who haven't been vaccinated and live outside are much more likely to get it than indoor pets.

Rabies is always an emergency—not just for the dog who has it, but for people and other pets who may be exposed. It's critical to call your veterinarian if you suspect any dog has rabies, says Dr. Lyon.

they're getting sick. Other symptoms of poisoning include vomiting, loss of balance, and breathing difficulties. Treatments for poisoning are usually very effective—but only if you get help right away.

The Best Care

Take a good look. It's usually not difficult to see objects that are wedged in the mouth, especially when you look inside with a small flashlight. The spots to check are between the teeth, around the gum line, under the tongue, and on the roof of the mouth. As long as your dog will let you do it, you can remove small objects with your fingers or a strong pair of tweezers. It's hard to hold your dog's mouth open while you work inside, however, so you may want to give her a tennis ball to hold, which will help keep the mouth open.

The discomfort of having their mouths held open and fingers poking about may be too much for some dogs. If you can see something inside, but can't get it out, call your vet.

Reach for a towel. Most of the time, drooling is just what dogs do. "Get used to it and keep towels handy," says Lillian Roberts, D.V.M., a veterinarian in private practice in Palm Desert, California, and author of *Emergency Vet: True Stories from the Animal Emergency Clinic.*

FAST FIX Some dogs suffer from car sickness. It's hard to stop nausea once it begins, but you can often prevent it by giving dogs dimenhydrinate (Dramamine) about an hour before a trip—12.5 milligrams for small dogs and 25 to 50 milligrams for medium to large dogs. Dramamine is safe for most dogs, but it shouldn't be given to those with glaucoma or bladder problems without a vet's supervision.

Ear Discharge

Dogs' ears are designed for protection. Rather than having a straight, horizontal canal leading to the eardrum, their ear canals have an L-shaped bend. This design helps prevent damage to the eardrum from foreign bodies getting into the ear canal, but it also provides a perfect pocket for wax, moisture, and debris as well as bacteria and other organisms that cause infections and discharges.

The Usual Suspects

Water in the ears. Bacteria and yeast thrive in the presence of moisture, and wet, humid ears provide an ideal home. Dogs with a brown, green, or white discharge, possibly with a little blood mixed in, almost certainly

have an infection and may need a course of antibiotics to knock it out, says Bernadine Cruz, D.V.M., a veterinarian in private practice in Laguna Hills, California.

Allergies. Some dogs develop discharges only in the spring and summer. In part this is because these are the swimming seasons, but it's also due to allergies. Dogs with hay fever sometimes get waxy, itchy ears, which can get inflamed and oozy, says Dr. Cruz.

Foreign objects. Anything that irritates the ears can produce a discharge. Dogs who spend a lot of time outside sometimes get twigs, burrs, or even

Dogs who spend a lot of time in the water often get ear infections. Shaking gives momentary relief, but won't stop the irritation.

AN UNEXPECTED RISK

Since ear infections can be painful, veterinarians often recommend treating them with antibiotics. In some cases, however, the treatment itself produces a discharge.

"If your pet's ears ooze after you start the treatment, she could be allergic to the antibiotic," says Jay W. Geasling, D.V.M., a veterinarian in private practice in Buffalo. This usually occurs with ointments containing the antibiotic neomycin, he explains.

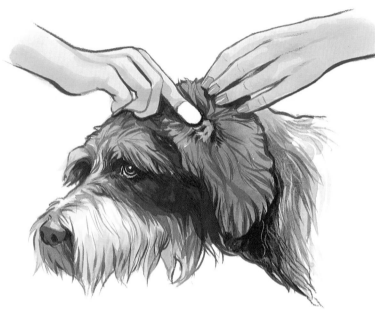

changes the pH in the ears, creating a less favorable environment for infections. If a dog has sores or cuts in the ear, just use vinegar and water, he advises. "The alcohol can burn the ear if there are any open sores, and if it hurts too much, your dog won't let you near the ears again." When you're done flushing the ears, dry the insides with a scrap of gauze.

People whose dogs spend a lot of time in the water sometimes flush their dogs' ears regularly to ensure that infections don't get started, explains Dr. Martin. Once a dog has an infection, however, you'll want to call your vet if it doesn't go away within a few days.

You can prevent infections by periodically flushing out the ear canal and drying it gently with a scrap of gauze wrapped around your finger.

stones inside the ear canal. Even worse are fox-tail seeds. Equipped with tiny barbs, the seeds can penetrate soft skin, causing a discharge along with pain and infection.

The Best Care

Remove the moisture. Whether or not your dog has been in the water, the insides of the ears are very humid. Drying them slightly will make them less hospitable to organisms causing a discharge. Bill Martin, D.V.M., a veterinarian in private practice in Fletcher, North Carolina, recommends mixing equal parts vinegar, rubbing alcohol, and water and running the solution through the ear canal with a bulb syringe. The alcohol will kill bacteria, and the vinegar

BREED SPECIFIC

Dogs with large, heavy ears, such as basset hounds and bloodhounds, are prone to ear infections because their ears aren't well-ventilated. Cocker spaniels, poodles, and schnauzers have a high risk of getting infections because of their remarkably hairy ears. All of the water dogs, such as Labrador retrievers and Irish setters (right), are at risk for ear problems, too.

Keep the water out. Rather than letting infections get started and having to fight them afterward, Dr. Cruz recommends putting cotton balls in the ears before your dog goes into water or before you wash her head.

"Put cotton balls in the ear, hold the ear flap down, wash that side, then repeat on the other side," she says.

Treat the allergies. It's impossible to avoid pollens entirely, but dogs with hay fever usually have fewer symptoms when you reduce their exposure somewhat. This may mean going for walks in sparsely landscaped city parks rather than country fields, although that's hardly a perfect solution. Keeping dogs inside the house during peak pollen times, usually early morning and in the evening, can help quite a bit. Once they're inhaling less pollen, the ear problems may start clearing up in a few days.

Dogs with food allergies occasionally have ear problems, too. If the discharges are happening in the winter as well as the spring and summer, talk to your vet about testing for allergies. Your dog may need to go on a special diet for a few weeks to help identify what she may be allergic to.

Remove ear hair. Some dogs have generous amounts of hair growing in their ears, which traps wax, grit, and moisture. Dr. Martin recommends using tweezers to pluck tufts of hair from the ear canal, being careful not to push the tweezers in too far toward the eardrum. Tweezing hair is uncomfortable and usually goes more smoothly when you remove just a little bit of hair at a time and spread the process out over a few days. Don't use depilatory creams because the tissues of the ear are too tender to withstand the chemical assault, he adds.

FAST FIX The infections that cause discharges can be painful, and some dogs will spend hours scratching their ears and shaking their heads to try and ease the pain. You can help by applying a few drops of Campho-Phenique, says Dr. Cruz. "It acts as a local anesthetic and will give temporary relief until you can get your dog to the vet," she says.

Before bathing a dog, plug her ears with cotton balls to keep moisture out of the ear canal.

Eye-Color Changes

Regardless of the color of their coats, most dogs have dark-colored eyes. The eyes are covered by a layer of cells called the cornea, which allows light to pass through to the lens beneath. Normally, both the cornea and the lens are transparent. But there are a number of conditions that can cause these complex layers of cells to take on a gray, cloudy, or bluish hue.

The Usual Suspects

Dry eyes. The color of the eyes is affected by the amount of tears the eyes produce. It is common for the eyes to become somewhat drier with the passing years. When tear production declines, it may cause a bluish color in the cornea, the surface of the eye.

Glaucoma. This is a serious condition in which fluid accumulates inside the eye, increasing pressure within the eyeball and impairing a dog's ability to see, says Christopher J. Murphy, D.V.M., associate professor of ophthalmology at the University of Wisconsin

Dogs with cataracts will have a bluish, cloudy look to their eyes.

School of Veterinary Medicine in Madison. Glaucoma may occur on its own or following an injury to the eye. One clue to look for is a layer of blue across the eye's surface that obscures the pupil beneath.

Cataracts. As pets age, the lenses of the eyes often start to harden a little and begin blocking small amounts of light. This condition, called cataracts, causes the eyes to get cloudy, possibly with a gray, blue, or bluish white color.

Pets with diabetes are particularly prone to cataracts, adds Dr. Murphy.

Nuclear sclerosis. This is another condition that often accompanies aging. The eyes are very efficient at creating new cells, but they aren't so good at getting rid of old ones. As the old cells build up in the lens, the lens becomes quite dense. Nuclear sclerosis has little effect on vision, but it does cause the pupils to take on a slight blue tint.

Corneal scratch. When one eye has turned slightly blue, and your pet is also squinting or has bloodshot eyes, there is a good chance that he has a scratch on the cornea, says Nancy

Willerton, D.V.M., a veterinarian in private practice in Denver.

The Best Care

Keep the eyes moist. Dogs with dry eyes need the same treatment people do—a few drops of artificial tears, available in drugstores, given once or twice a day. This usually takes care of the problem, although dogs with more serious symptoms may need surgery to restore the normal flow of tears.

Block the sun. The eyes are surprisingly hardy given their delicate construction, and corneal scratches will usually heal quite nicely on their own, says Dr. Willerton. But the eye will be very sore and sensitive to light in the meantime, so you may want to pick up a sun-blocking visor at the pet supply store.

"If the eye seems no better in a day, get your veterinarian to check it out," Dr. Willerton adds.

Make life predictable. Even though most eye-color changes don't result in blindness, they can still make it harder for dogs to see.

"Pets with poor eyesight memorize the layout of your home, so it is better not to rearrange the furniture too often," says Dr. Willerton. She also recommends keeping the floors clear of unexpected objects. A pile of books is easy for you to avoid, but pets with failing vision may walk

CALL FOR HELP

While dogs that develop bluish eyes generally experience nothing worse than a slight loss of vision, dogs with cloudy eyes need to be seen by a veterinarian right away. Glaucoma often turns the eyes cloudy, and it can cause blindness very quickly if left untreated. Eye infections can also cause the eyes to turn cloudy, as can internal problems such as high blood pressure and cancer.

"A cloudy eye should always be considered an emergency situation that needs a vet," says Christopher J. Murphy, D.V.M., associate professor of ophthalmology at the University of Wisconsin School of Veterinary Medicine in Madison.

A sun visor doesn't just look snappy, it's a great way to block the sun's glare and prevent further damage to sore eyes.

right into them. Flights of stairs are hazardous, too, and are best blocked off with a baby gate. It needs to be of sufficient height, though, to prevent a dog from jumping over.

Get a checkup, then relax. Eye color changes should always be checked by a veterinarian, but most of the time, you won't have to do much of anything because they're just a part of aging—and because dogs' other senses are so sharp that they don't need 20/20 vision. In fact, it's common for dogs to have cataracts or other minor vision problems for years before anyone even notices, says Dr. Willerton.

Eye Discharge

Dogs' eyes are awash in watery tears that clean and lubricate the surfaces of the eyes. It's normal for tears to leave behind moist or sticky deposits. These are the "sleepers" that you'll often see at the corners of their eyes.

Even though some tearing is normal, veterinarians get nervous when dogs start producing more tears than usual or when there's discharge that's thick or green. Most eye problems aren't serious and will clear up on their own, but they can cause a lot of discomfort in the meantime. More worrisome is the fact that some eye injuries and infections can cause permanent damage if they aren't treated quickly. A discharge from one eye is less likely to be serious than a discharge from both, says Christine Wilford, D.V.M., a veterinarian in private practice in Edmonds, Washington. Play safe and call your vet if a discharge doesn't get better within a day or two, she advises. If the problem isn't serious, your vet may suggest irrigating the eyes several times day with saline solution to help heal minor injuries or soothe mild eye irritation.

The Usual Suspects

Corneal damage. The transparent surface of the eyeball, called the cornea, is easily scratched by such things as low-hanging branches, dust, and even grass seeds. The scratches usually heal fairly quickly, but they can cause a heavy watery discharge in the meantime. There may be a discharge when

bits of debris get stuck behind the third eyelid, a thin membrane that's attached to the inner corners of dogs' eyes.

While some eye injuries and infections heal quickly on their own, an inflammation of the cornea, called keratitis, may cause blindness if left untreated, says Dr. Wilford. Dogs that have keratitis will have a discharge and also a whitish discoloration on the clear part of the eye. They'll be squinting as well, says Dr. Wilford.

Pinkeye. The inner surfaces of the eyelids are covered with a gossamer-thin membrane called the conjunctiva. Anything that irritates the conjunctiva, such as allergies or infections, will make the eyes red and irritated—a condition called conjunctivitis, or pinkeye. In addition, the inside of the lower eyelid will be red, and you may be able to see large blood vessels across the white of the eye, says Dr. Wilford.

"Many dogs have mild allergies during the pollen season," says Bonnie Wilcox, D.V.M., a veterinarian in private practice in Preemption,

BREED SPECIFIC

Pugs, bulldogs (below), and Pekingese are more at risk of eye irritation than most breeds because their facial hair, instead of growing away from the eye, sometimes grows toward it, causing irritation and occasionally infection.

Illinois. They can be allergic to many of the same things as people, such as tree or grass pollens. Dogs with allergies often get a little itchy, and the combination of red, watery eyes and an overactive hind leg usually means a dog has an allergy, she says. Pinkeye that's caused by viral or bacterial infections is highly contagious and can easily pass from dog to dog.

Dry eye. Most dogs produce all the tears they need, but some older dogs get a condition called dry eye, or keratoconjunctivitis sicca, which stops them from making enough tears. This makes the eyes dry and irritated and produces a thick, sticky discharge, says Dr. Wilcox.

Entropion. Some dogs are born with a curious condition called entropion, in which the eyelids don't fit as firmly against the eyeball as they should. The loose fit allows the eyelids to turn inward, or invert. When this happens, the eyelashes brush against the surface of the eyeball, causing irritation and a discharge, says Dr. Wilcox. Surgery to tighten the loose lids is the only permanent treatment for entropion, but it can't be done until a dog is fully grown. Your vet may prescribe medicated eye drops to keep the eyes as comfortable as possible until your dog is ready for surgery.

The Best Care

Bathe the eyes. Regardless of what's causing the discharge, bathing your dog's eyes with preservative-free saline or contact-lens solution relieves itching and irritation quickly and also helps flush out irritating particles, says Dr. Wilford. Put a drop or two of the solution into each eye. When your dog blinks, the solution will

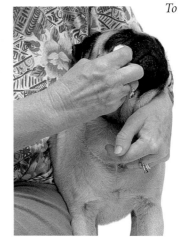

To stop discharges from building up and irritating this pug's eyes, his owner wipes them every day with a soft, moist cloth.

spread completely over the surface of the eyes, she explains. You can repeat this treatment several times a day.

For dogs that have mild cases of pinkeye, an alternative to saline solution is a dilute solution of boric acid, specially prepared for ophthalmic use. Available in drugstores, the solution cleans the eyes and acts as a mild antiseptic.

Clean away the discharge. It's not a good idea to let any kind of eye discharge accumulate because it can irritate tender tissues around the eyes. Discharges are easy to remove if you swab them every day with a damp cloth or cotton wool, says Dr. Wilford. Don't use soap, however, because it will sting.

Stop the scratching and rubbing. Dogs deal with irritated eyes the best way they can, which usually involves pawing them or rubbing them on carpets or furniture. All this rubbing provides temporary relief, but it also usually aggravates the underlying problem, says Dr. Wilford. Most veterinarians recommend fitting a dog with an Elizabethan collar, a cone-shaped

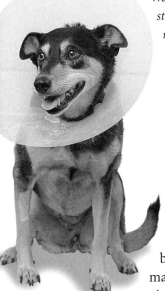

Wearing an Elizabethan collar stops this dog from pawing and rubbing at her sore eyes.

hood that helps to protect the eyes until they have a chance to heal.

Keep them quiet. Eye irritations are often slow to heal because the eyes are open to the elements. Dogs who spend much of their time outside get a lot of sunlight, wind, and debris in their eyes, and this makes the tissues drier and more irritated, says Dr. Wilford. She recommends avoiding vigorous exercise until the discharge is gone and the eyes have recovered. When you do take your dog outside, you may want to fit her with a pair of eyeshades, available in pet supply stores.

Irrigate the eyes. Dry eye needs veterinary treatment with prescription drugs. The vet will probably also recommend artificial tears, available from drug stores, that you can squeeze into your dog's eyes several times a day to help ease the discomfort of dry eye.

Preserve the evidence. Since the eyes are so delicate, see your vet when discharges don't clear up within a few days. "Don't wash the eyes before taking your dog in," Dr. Wilford says. "Your vet will need to see the discharge to know what's causing the problem and what the best treatment will be."

Every eye problem is different, she adds, and medications that work for one eye problem can be dangerous when used for another. It's a good idea to talk to your vet before putting anything stronger than saline in your dog's eyes, she says.

FAST FIX Even a slight eye discharge can be a problem for dogs with a lot of hair around their eyes. The hair traps eye fluids that attract dust and debris, causing dry, gritty accumulations that can irritate the eye and lead to infections. Keep the hair clean and combed or trimmed short with blunt-ended scissors to help the tears drain away from the eyes, says Dr. Wilcox.

A CRYING SHAME

Dogs always shed tears, but they usually aren't visible because of the darkness of their coats. White dogs, however, sometimes develop tear "trails"—dark streaks that form under the eyes when pigments in tears, called porphyrins, oxidize and dry into red or brownish streaks, says Christine Wilford, D.V.M., a veterinarian in private practice in Edmonds, Washington. Porphyrins are totally harmless, but they're difficult to clean off, if only because it's hard to wash around a dog's eyes. Keeping hair around the eyes trimmed short and wiping around the eyes once a day will help prevent the stains from forming, says Dr. Wilford. In addition, you can buy a product called Crystal Eye in pet supply stores, which helps remove the stains without irritating the eyes.

Eye Redness

The white of the eye (the sclera) is networked with tiny blood vessels. Red, bloodshot eyes mean that something has damaged the vessels, causing them to swell. This is rarely serious, but some internal problems and injuries may cause redness, so you'll want to call your vet when it doesn't go away within a day or two, says Anna Scholey, D.V.M., a veterinarian in private practice in Dallas.

You can tell right away if redness is caused by injuries or illnesses. Internal problems will usually cause redness in both eyes, while injuries usually affect one eye or the other.

The Usual Suspects

Trapped debris. Dogs have a structure called the third eyelid, which is designed to protect the eyes. What sometimes happens is that this "extra" eyelid traps splinters, grass seeds, or other debris and scrapes it across the surface of the eye, says Paul M. Gigliotti, D.V.M., a veterinarian in private practice in Mayfield Village, Ohio. "A foreign body in the eye is the most common cause of bloodshot eyes," he explains.

Allergies. Dogs with hay fever often get red eyes in spring and summer, when pollen counts are high. In cooler weather, dust and mold spores can produce allergies and red eyes in susceptible dogs.

Joy-riding. Dogs' idea of heaven is to ride in cars with the windows wide open, their heads outside, and their ears plastered back by the wind. The rush of air brings them a world of

Dogs love riding in the backs of trucks, but wind and airborne debris can cause red, irritated eyes.

exciting smells, but it also dries and irritates the eyes and is a common cause of redness.

Infections. Eye infections can crop up on their own or when something irritates the eye and makes it easier for harmful organisms to get in, says Dr. Gigliotti. Many infections affect the conjunctiva, a thin layer of tissue that covers the inside of the eyelids. Dogs with conjunctivitis, or pinkeye, often have a watery discharge along with the redness.

The Best Care

Flush the eyes. Whether redness is caused by allergies or debris, veterinarians recommend flushing the eyes with saline solution, available

79

A warm compress gently applied to a red eye will help reduce the inflammation and pain.

in drugstores. This soothes the eyes and also removes debris that may be too small for you to see, says Dr. Scholey. Here's how to do it.

• Fill a bulb syringe or turkey baster with saline solution.

• Tip your dog's head back and use your thumb and forefinger to hold the eye open.

• Direct a gentle stream of water over the surface of the eye. When you're done, use cotton wool or a clean tissue to swab the excess fluid.

Eyes will often return to their normal color within a day after the flushing. If they don't, there's probably another problem and you'll want to call your vet, says Dr. Scholey.

Ask about antibiotics. Since eye redness is often caused by infections, your veterinarian may recommend using an ophthalmic antibiotic ointment. Antibiotics can relieve symptoms in as little as a day, although you may have to continue using ointment for up to a week to eliminate the underlying infection. Antibiotics only work against bacteria, however, not against viruses or other organisms. You'll need to check with your vet before using the ointments at home, says Dr. Scholey.

 FAST FIX Dogs with wind- or sunburned eyes will quickly recover when you apply a warm compress. Dip a washcloth in warm water, wring it out, and hold it against your dog's eyes for a few minutes once a day. The gentle heat improves blood flow, which can help the eyes recover more quickly.

CALL FOR HELP

The eyes are filled with fluids that constantly flow around the tissues. As dogs get older, however, the tiny pores through which fluid flows out of the eyes may become clogged, causing pressure inside the eye to rise. This condition, called glaucoma, can damage the eyes very quickly and is usually treated with prescription medications.

Glaucoma usually comes on slowly, but veterinarians sometimes see dogs with "fast" glaucoma, which can occur in just a few days, says Christopher J. Murphy, D.V.M., associate professor of ophthalmology at the University of Wisconsin School of Veterinary Medicine in Madison.

A dog whose eyes are normal one day and red and bulging the next needs to see a veterinarian immediately, says Dr. Murphy. This is especially true if you have an elderly dog, or a cocker spaniel or basset hound, who are prone to the fast type of glaucoma.

Fainting

Dogs don't faint when they get excited or frightened. But they may faint when the flow of oxygen to the brain temporarily slows or stops—either because something is physically blocking the flow of air into the lungs, or because blood, which carries oxygen throughout the body, isn't getting through to the brain for some reason.

The Usual Suspects

Heart problems. The most common cause of fainting is probably heart disease, specifically a condition called heart block, which causes a sudden interruption of the electrical signals to the heart, says Karen Zagorsky, D.V.M., a veterinarian in private practice in Moreno Valley, California.

Airway obstruction. Dogs who have gotten something stuck in their windpipes may not be able to pull in enough oxygen to supply the brain. This can be a particular problem in dogs like boxers, bulldogs, and pugs, whose windpipes tend to be narrower than those of other breeds, says Dr. Zagorsky.

Chemical fumes. Some dogs are sensitive to the fumes from paint and other chemicals—and any dog may faint when the concentration of fumes is great enough. Fumes that are strong enough to cause fainting may be strong enough to damage the lungs, so you'll need to see your veterinarian right away.

Accidents and illnesses. It's not uncommon for dogs with head injuries to faint—sometimes days or weeks after the injury occurred. Dogs with epilepsy may have occasional fainting spells. So will dogs with diabetes whose blood sugar has plunged too low, says

OUT OF BALANCE

It doesn't happen very often, but sometimes a dog will suddenly fall over and begin rolling on the ground. It may look as though he fainted for a moment, but what probably happened is that his body's balance center suddenly lost its moorings.

A mysterious condition called idiopathic vestibular disease affects the part of the nervous system (the vestibular system) that controls balance. Dogs who have this condition may feel fine one moment, then suddenly lose their balance, says Stephen A. Smith, D.V.M., a veterinarian in private practice in Pasadena, Maryland.

Veterinarians still don't know what causes idiopathic vestibular disease. At one time they thought it was caused by eating blue-tailed lizards—until they discovered that most pets who get the condition have never seen a blue-tailed lizard, much less eaten one. They now suspect that it's caused by a chemical imbalance in fluids in the inner ear.

Even though the attacks look scary, they're usually not serious, and most dogs will feel fine within three to five days.

Nanette Westhof, D.V.M., a veterinarian in private practice in Mesa, Arizona.

Narcolepsy. Dogs with a neurological condition called narcolepsy can suddenly collapse and fall into a deep sleep without any warning at all. Narcolepsy usually isn't dangerous, although a dog who falls asleep on the edge of the stairs may find himself taking a tumble. There isn't a cure for narcolepsy, but it can usually be treated with medications.

The Best Care

Check for air flow. A dog who has fainted could be seriously ill, but before you call your veterinarian, there are a few things to check; the information you give will help your vet figure out what's going on.

• Look at the color of the dog's gums. "If they're pale or have a bluish color, that means there's not enough oxygen getting to the brain," says Lynn Harpold, D.V.M., a veterinarian in private practice in Mesa, Arizona.

• Feel for a heart beat. The best place to find a dog's pulse is on the inner thigh, near where it meets the body. If there isn't a pulse you'll need to get your dog to a veterinarian as soon as you can. It can take as little as five minutes for lack of oxygen to cause irreversible brain damage, so even before you can get to the vet, you'll need to get his breathing started again. For an illustrated description of how to perform artificial respiration on dogs, see page 45.

• Look inside the mouth to see if something's blocking the windpipe. If there is an obstruction, either remove it or perform the

Dogs faint when there isn't enough oxygen getting to the brain. A quick test is to look at the gums. They should be bubble-gum pink. Pale or bluish gums mean the body isn't getting all the oxygen it needs.

Heimlich maneuver to dislodge it. See page 50 for more information on doing the Heimlich maneuver. Be careful about reaching into your dog's mouth because you could get bitten, Dr. Harpold adds. If there's time, pull on a pair of heavy gloves to protect your hands before reaching inside.

Give him some fresh air. A dog who suddenly keels over while you're painting the living room was probably overwhelmed by the fumes. About the best thing you can do is get him outside where he can breathe some fresh air. Dogs who have fainted may recover quite quickly as long as there isn't something seriously wrong. But you'll want to call your vet to be sure.

Fever

While prolonged high temperatures can be dangerous, most dogs cope with fevers just fine. In fact, fevers may be helpful because they make it more difficult for germs to thrive inside the body.

"Fever is part of the body's healing process," says Tim Banker, D.V.M, a veterinarian in private practice in Greensboro, North Carolina. "People are often too quick to try to mask the symptom, rather than realizing that it's the body's attempt to take care of itself."

Of course, even a slight fever can make dogs hot and miserable, which is why many veterinarians recommend lowering the heat when their temperatures rise above 102.5°F.

The Usual Suspects

Infections. Dogs with fevers nearly always have a bacterial or viral infection—from a cold, for example, or a bout with the flu. Don't bother feeling your dog's forehead, however. Since dogs naturally run hotter than people, you can't use this method to tell if their temperatures are running above normal. The only way to tell is to take their temperature with a rectal thermometer.

Hyperthermia. When it comes to generating heat, the body acts like the engine of a car. Dogs who have been "turned on," either because of exercise or excitement, will often run a few degrees warmer than usual. And because dogs don't dispel body heat as effectively as people do, they may pant heavily or seem unusually tired for a long time afterward. This type of

P O O C H   P U Z Z L E R

Can you detect a fever by feeling your dog's nose?

A cool, moist nose is often believed to be a sign of good health, while a warm nose is thought to mean a dog is sick. While it would be nice if you could diagnose fever just by feeling your dog's nose, it really doesn't work, says Bernadine Cruz, D.V.M., a veterinarian in private practice in Laguna Hills, California.

"A moist nose is an indication of nothing but a moist nose," she says. Dogs with fever sometimes have a dry, warm nose. But they're just as likely to have a wet nose. The only accurate way to diagnose a fever in a dog is, unfortunately, the old-fashioned way—with a rectal thermometer.

"fever" isn't a problem, of course—unless a dog gets so hot that her body temperature rises above 104°F, a condition known as heatstroke. Dogs with heatstroke need to see a veterinarian immediately, says Dr. Banker.

The Best Care

Watch where your dog goes. Dogs with fevers will instinctively seek out cold surfaces to help lower their temperatures. Spending as little as a half-hour in a cool place can lower their temperatures by as much as 1 degree—enough to make a big difference in how they feel. You can help your dog get better a little

When dogs' temperatures are higher than normal, they'll often lie in a cool place, such as on a linoleum floor, in order to cool themselves down.

more quickly by trusting her instincts and letting her rest wherever she feels comfortable.

Of course, dogs with fevers don't always feel warm—sometimes they get chills as well. Don't be surprised if you find your pet curled up on the bathroom floor in the morning and next to the radiator at night.

Lower fever with aspirin. Perhaps the easiest way to lower fever is to give dogs buffered or coated aspirin. Lila Miller, D.V.M., senior director of animal sciences and veterinary adviser to the American Society for the Prevention of Cruelty to Animals in New York City, recommends giving one-quarter of a 325 milligram tablet for every 20 pounds of weight, once or twice a day.

Some dogs are sensitive to aspirin, however, so check with your veterinarian before giving it at home. And don't substitute related medications such as acetaminophen or ibuprofen, which can be dangerous for dogs, Dr. Miller says.

Taking a Dog's Temperature

Oral thermometers won't work with dogs because they tend to bite the glass. Ear-probe thermometers don't work either because dogs have an L-shaped ear canal that makes it difficult for signals from the thermometers to bounce off the eardrum. The only effective way to take their temperature is with a rectal thermometer.

Lubricate the thermometer with petroleum jelly. Then insert it about halfway into the rectum. Leave it there for about three minutes, then wipe it clean and take the reading. Dogs normally run between 99.5°F and 102.5°F. Anything warmer means your dog has a fever.

CALL FOR HELP

Even though fever is a natural part of the body's healing process, it may be a sign of serious problems—anything from Lyme disease to cancer. Veterinarians worry most about fever in very young or very old dogs because they tend to be frail and can become dehydrated quite easily.

Most fevers wind down fairly quickly, but if your pet stays feverish for more than a day, or she's having other symptoms such as vomiting or loss of appetite, you'll want to call your veterinarian right away.

Try an herbal cure. The herb echinacea is renowned for its ability to help the body fight infection. It won't stop fever quickly, but by helping the body cope with the underlying problem, it may bring the fever down naturally. Veterinarians familiar with herbal cures recommend giving dogs 12 to 20 drops of a low-alcohol or nonalcohol echinacea tincture for every 20 pounds of weight, two or three times a day.

Give them plenty of water. Dogs who are overheating can lose essential fluids and become dehydrated very quickly, so be sure to provide more water than usual. If your dog doesn't want to drink, you may need to help out by filling a turkey baster or bulb syringe with water and squirting a little into the side of her mouth. Don't squirt it toward the back of her mouth because it might get into the lungs.

For an added boost, you can replace the water with a little Pedialyte, which helps restore essential minerals called electrolytes that often run low in pets who have fevers.

FAST FIX A quick way to lower a fever is to lay a wet towel on your dog's belly, says Bernadine Cruz, D.V.M., a veterinarian in private practice in Laguna Hills, California. For larger dogs, it may be helpful to gently hose them down in the yard for a minute or two, she adds.

Another way to lower fever is to soak a cotton ball in isopropyl alcohol and apply it to the tummy for a few seconds. Alcohol evaporates almost instantly, which is what makes the skin feel cool, says Dr. Cruz. Be sure not to apply it to inflamed skin, though, because it will sting.

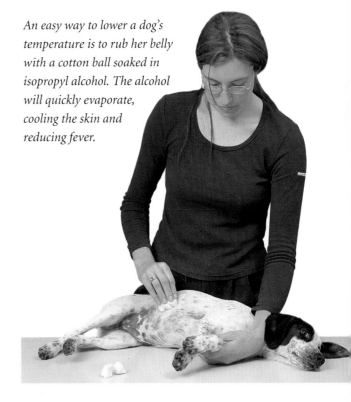

An easy way to lower a dog's temperature is to rub her belly with a cotton ball soaked in isopropyl alcohol. The alcohol will quickly evaporate, cooling the skin and reducing fever.

Flatulence

The digestive tract is full of enzymes and bacteria that the body uses to transform kibble into energy. A little gas is a completely natural part of this process. When dogs are unusually flatulent, however, or the smell is particularly foul, something is throwing the bowel out of balance.

The Usual Suspects

Worms. "A gassy pet is often infested with worms," says John Brooks, D.V.M., a veterinarian in private practice in Fork, Maryland. Most common are tapeworms and roundworms, which irritate the lining of the intestine and interfere with proper digestion. Visible as white specks or spaghetti-like strands in the stool, these worms usually aren't dangerous, but you don't want to ignore them, either, as they can cause other problems apart from gas.

Unauthorized foods. Dogs don't always discriminate between open garbage cans and their food dishes, and spoiled, smelly food certainly won't be sweeter when it wafts into the air hours after a garbage raid.

Commercial foods. Most commercial pet foods contain beans, bran, whole wheat, and fat, all of which are difficult for digestive enzymes to break down. Foods that don't break down entirely will collect in the colon and ferment, causing large amounts of gas.

Food allergies. Dogs who are allergic to ingredients in their food—soy protein is often a problem—won't be able to digest efficiently and

CALL FOR HELP

Even though flatulence is so common that veterinarians are more likely to joke about it than worry about it, a sudden increase in gas that doesn't improve within a few days must be checked out by a veterinarian.

To save time and help your vet work more quickly, collect a fresh stool sample before you leave the house, adds John Brooks, D.V.M., a veterinarian in private practice in Fork, Maryland. This will allow your veterinarian to check for worms and other parasites as well as for undigested fats—a sign of pancreatic problems.

will often be very gassy, says Dr. Brooks. They may have diarrhea as well.

To see if something in your dog's diet is responsible, write down everything he had to eat in the 24 hours preceding the gassy episodes, suggests Jim Hendrickson, V.M.D., a veterinarian in emergency private practice in Rockville, Maryland. Sometimes something as simple as switching to a different brand of treats will help dogs smell a little better.

Swallowing air. Air gets into the digestive tract all the time without anyone noticing and without causing too many problems. Dogs who gobble their food too quickly, however, can swallow huge amounts of air. The air has to go somewhere—and out it goes, many times a day.

Pancreatic disease. The pancreas is the organ that produces digestive enzymes. Dogs who have pancreatic disease or other internal problems such as intestinal viruses or cancer will often have a lot of flatulence, says Dr. Brooks. An increase in flatulence that's accompanied by loose stools and weight loss is a serious warning sign that needs to be checked by a veterinarian, he advises. If it turns out that your dog does have pancreatic problems, there's a good chance he'll be just fine as long as you give him digestive enzymes to replace the ones the body isn't able to make.

The Best Solutions

Switch to a bowel-friendly diet. To find out if food is causing the fumes, give your dog easy-to-digest foods such as cottage cheese and boiled rice for a few days, says Dr. Hendrickson. If the air clears, you may want to make a permanent change. One commercial food that's very digestible is Hill's Science Diet Prescription Diet I/D. Or check with your veterinarian about other foods, either homemade or store-bought, that may help.

Extend the dinner hour. You can reduce the amount of air that dogs swallow by giving them three or four small meals a day instead of one big meal, says Joanne Hibbs, D.V.M., a veterinarian in private practice in Powell, Tennessee. If you've got more than one dog, try feeding them separately. Otherwise, they'll often gulp their food down to make sure that the other one doesn't get it first.

Ask about an elimination diet. Food allergies are easy to treat: Stop giving your dog foods that he's sensitive to and the symptoms will go away. Things get complicated because most dogs eat dozens of different things a day, ranging from the variety of proteins in their food to the flavorings of rawhide treats. Your vet will help you plan a diet called an elimination diet, which makes it easy to see which, if any, ingredients your dog is reacting to.

FAST FIX Veterinarians sometimes recommend giving gassy dogs a product called CurTail. Available from vets, it contains digestive enzymes that help the intestines work more efficiently. Adolph's Meat Tenderizer has a similar effect. "That's usually what I try first," says Dr. Brooks. He recommends using a half-teaspoon of Adolph's per cup of food, mixing it in, and letting it sit for 10 minutes to give it time to work.

Dogs who are fed from communal bowls will often gulp their food to avoid missing out. To cut the competition— and the resulting gulping and gassing—give each dog his own bowl.

Foot-Licking

It looks like a quirk of breeding, but that's not the reason some white dogs have dark front feet. They look like they're wearing socks because they lick their feet. Chemical reactions between saliva, oxygen, and fur can turn the feet a rusty color.

Light-colored dogs can't hide their secret passion, but foot-licking is a popular activity among almost all dogs. Most get by with a lick-and-polish, but some act obsessed and will lick their paws at every opportunity, sometimes for hours at a stretch, says Lila Miller, D.V.M., senior director of animal sciences and veterinary adviser to the American Society for the Prevention of Cruelty to Animals in New York City.

The Usual Suspects

Allergies. Common in toy breeds, allergies such as hay fever can irritate the skin and make it itchy, says Dr. Miller. The feet don't necessarily get itchier than other parts of the body, but veterinarians have found that dogs who are allergic to pollen, mold, or dust often focus on their feet and legs, which are easy to reach.

Boredom. Dogs who get bored easily and don't have a lot to do may turn to foot-licking as a way of passing the time and dispelling nervous energy, says Dr. Miller. In addition, some dogs develop a condition called obsessive-compulsive

All dogs lick their feet sometimes, but constant licking can be a symptom of allergies, sore feet, or boredom.

disorder, in which they can't quit doing certain things, such as licking their feet or biting their tails. Giving dogs more attention and exercise will take care of boredom and take their minds off their feet, says Dr. Miller. Obsessive-compulsive disorder, however, is much more serious and needs to be treated by an expert.

Pad cuts and cracks. The paw pads are tough and resilient, but they're also slow to heal when they get damaged. Dogs treat pad problems the same way they treat any other injury, which is to give them a thorough licking.

Hair mats. Dogs have a lot of hair between their toes, and it's not uncommon for the hairs to bind together in tough little mats. Hair mats are irritating, and dogs will spend hours trying to bite them free and relieve the irritation.

The Best Care

Add supplements to the diet. Veterinarians are finding that dogs are itchier overall than they used to be, and they suspect that part of the reason is that heavily processed commercial

DANGEROUS SORES

Dogs like to lick, and it usually isn't a big deal. When they do it too long and too often, however, they can develop painful wounds called lick granulomas—red, circular sores that can be very slow to heal and often get infected, says Lila Miller, D.V.M., senior director of animal sciences and veterinary adviser to the American Society for the Prevention of Cruelty to Animals in New York City.

Once lick granulomas have developed, getting rid of them is a challenge. Moisturizers can help, and triple antibiotic cream may stop infection. But lick granulomas don't always respond to home care. In most cases, you'll need to see your vet, says Dr. Miller.

Apply a foot softener. The paw pads usually don't crack or chafe unless they're drier than they should be. A quick way to lubricate the pads is to apply a lotion containing lanolin once a day until they're soft and supple. Don't apply the lotion for more than a few weeks, however. The paw pads need to be tough to give protection, says Dr. Miller.

Clip the hair. For dogs who have hairy feet, trimming the hair between their toes with blunt-nosed scissors will help reduce the irritation, says Dr. Miller. This is especially helpful for indoor dogs, who don't always generate enough foot-friction to wear down the hair naturally.

FAST FIX Soaking a dog's feet in cool water is a quick way to reduce itching, says Dr. Wynn.

foods may not provide all the nutrients they need, says Susan Wynn, D.V.M., a veterinarian in private practice in Marietta, Georgia, and co-editor of *Complementary and Alternative Veterinary Medicine.* She recommends giving dogs vitamin C, which can help make the skin healthier. Dogs over 50 pounds can take 1,000 milligrams of vitamin C a day, says Dr. Wynn. Medium-size dogs can take 750 milligrams, and dogs 15 pounds or under can take 250 milligrams a day.

Another supplement that's good for the skin is fish oil, says Dr. Wynn. You can buy fish-oil capsules in pet supply and health food stores. She recommends giving dogs who weigh less than 15 pounds half a fish-oil capsule a day. Give one capsule to dogs weighing 15 to 34 pounds, two capsules to dogs 35 to 50 pounds, and three capsules to dogs over 50 pounds.

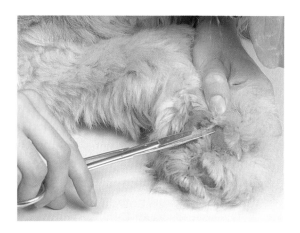

Regularly clipping the hair between your dog's toes will prevent irritating hair mats from forming.

Fur Loss

With the exception of a few hairless breeds, all dogs have smooth, even coats, no matter what their age. Most dogs shed heavily twice a year, in the spring and the fall. Shedding that's unusually heavy or out of season, or hair that's falling out in patches, means that something's either interfering with the hair's normal growth or is causing existing hairs to break off or fall out.

The Usual Suspects

Mites. A dog's hair follicles are normally occupied by tiny parasites called demodex mites. (They live on people, too, in the eyebrow follicles.) In small numbers, demodex mites are harmless, but when they multiply—which typically occurs when dogs are ill or the immune system is weaker than it should be—they can cause a lot of hair to fall out. The hair loss starts around the eyelids, the mouth, and the front legs, causing bare patches about an inch across.

Nutritional problems. Most dogs get all the protein and fatty acids that they need from their food. But some dogs fall short in nutritional requirements, either because they need more of these nutrients than other dogs do or because they're eating mainly human leftovers.

Nutritional shortfalls may cause a dog's hair to fall out, making the coat look thin and somewhat dull, says Craig N. Carter, D.V.M., Ph.D., head of epidemiology at the Texas Veterinary Medical Diagnostic Laboratory at Texas A&M University in College Station.

CALL FOR HELP

Anything that affects the balance of the body's hormones can make the coat look dry, dull, or patchy. One of the most common of these conditions is a thyroid deficiency called hypothyroidism.

Dogs with low levels of thyroid hormone will often lose fur in symmetrical patches on both sides of their bodies, says Anna Scholey, D.V.M., a veterinarian in private practice in Dallas. Other symptoms may include fatigue, changes in appetite, or changes in thirst or urinary habits.

Thyroid deficiences can be a real problem when they're not detected and treated. Once your vet knows what's wrong, however, the problem is easily treated by giving dogs thyroid supplements, which replenish the body's natural supply of thyroid hormone.

Stress. Dogs who are shedding heavily out of season are said to be blowing their coats, and it's often a sign of physical or emotional stress—when they've been ill, for example, or when their lives are disrupted in some way. Usually, however, the hair grows back quickly and the problem is short-lived.

Fleas. When dogs are scratching so hard that the fur is literally flying, there's a very good chance that fleas are the problem. Vigorous scratching not only releases hair that's ready to

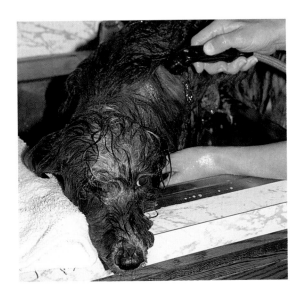

Most dogs don't need bathing very often, but those with seborrhea often need weekly baths as well as an oil-dissolving shampoo.

fall out anyway, it also breaks off healthy hairs, giving the skin a patchy appearance.

Seborrhea. Another itchy condition is seborrhea, in which the skin cells die and flake off much more quickly than normal and build up on the skin. Oils accumulate in this dense layer of dead cells, causing greasy, foul-smelling fur and bare patches that may resemble those caused by ringworm.

The Best Care

Check for ringworm. A quick way to tell when hair loss is caused by ringworm is to shine an ultraviolet light on your dog's coat. These lights, available from plant and garden stores, will often cause the infected areas to glow green. The test isn't always effective, however, so the lack of a green glow doesn't necessarily mean that a dog is free of ringworm. And other substances on a dog's fur, such as medications or natural skin oils, may also glow.

To get rid of ringworm, wear gloves and clip around the infected area with blunt-nosed scissors or clippers. Be careful not to touch yourself or other pets with the gloves or the clipped hair because ringworm is highly contagious—to people as well as to pets. Then wash your dog's entire body with an antifungal shampoo.

Get rid of mites. Demodex mites are rarely a serious problem and tend to quit causing trouble without any help from you. But in some cases, they cause bacterial infections that can in turn cause painful sores.

Washing your dog with a medicated shampoo will help control mild cases of demodex mites. More serious infestations usually require a veterinarian's help—mainly, regular dips with a powerful mite-killing solution.

BREED SPECIFIC

Some Arctic breeds, such as Siberian huskies and Alaskan malamutes (right), have a genetic tendency to absorb too little zinc. This can cause hair loss along with scaly, crusty patches on the skin. When these dogs take zinc supplements, however, their coats quickly return to normal.

Eliminate fleas. It's easy enough to recognize fleas, but it can take an army to get rid of them. Once your pet is infested, you might want to take a combination approach, using flea shampoos, powders, and possibly oral medications to get their numbers down.

Treating your home once a year with a product called Rx for Fleas will help eliminate fleas while also reducing the need for harmful chemicals, adds Susan Wynn, D.V.M., a veterinarian in private practice in Marietta, Georgia, and co-editor of *Complementary and Alternative Veterinary Medicine.*

Dissolve the oils. Even veterinarians have a hard time controlling seborrhea. About all you can do is wash your dog with an oil-dissolving shampoo, available in pet supply stores, whenever she starts getting greasy and itchy. Most dogs don't need baths very often, but those with seborrhea may need to be washed as often as once a week.

Regular baths can be helpful even for dogs without seborrhea, but whose coats are a little thinner than they should be, adds Anna Scholey, D.V.M., a veterinarian in private practice in Dallas. Washing and massaging the coat stimulates circulation and makes the skin healthier, she explains.

Buy a high-quality food. You don't have to spend a fortune on premium foods to keep the coat healthy, says Dr. Carter, but you do want to use a name-brand food, which will usually provide all the nutrients dogs need. In addition, your veterinarian may recommend giving supplements—either vitamins and minerals or fatty acids, which are good for the skin and coat. There's nothing wrong with using supplements

Frequent brushing helps keep the coat healthy by distributing natural oils and stimulating circulation.

at home, but you'll want to ask your veterinarian to recommend the proper combination, says Dan Carey, D.V.M., a veterinarian with the Iams pet food company in Dayton, Ohio.

"There's a precise balance between the omega-3 and omega-6 fatty acids," he says. "Adding the wrong oil or giving too much can throw the balance off."

Brush them often. Brushing your dog's coat once or twice a week does more than keep shed fur off the furniture. It also stimulates circulation and increases the production of oils that help protect the skin and coat.

Genital Discharge

Dogs get mild infections all the time, and their immune systems usually wipe them out long before symptoms appear. Once a genital discharge occurs, however, you can be pretty sure that an infection is well-established. The only exception to this is when female dogs are in heat, in which case a genital discharge is normal and will disappear on its own in a week or two.

A genital discharge means a dog is sick and needs to see a vet. The infections aren't always serious, however, and there are a number of things you can do to help your dog recover—or to prevent the infections in the first place.

The Usual Suspects

Urinary tract infection. In males especially, a blood-tinged genital discharge may mean they have an infection in the urethra, the tube that carries urine from the bladder and through the penis.

Less often, a bloody discharge may be caused by an injury to the penis. Females also get urinary tract infections, but the symptoms are more likely to be frequent or painful urination than a bloody discharge.

Prostate infection. The prostate gland supplies the fluid that makes up the semen, and when it gets infected it can cause a yellowish or bloody discharge from the penis.

Dogs with a prostate infection are often quite sick. Symptoms include abdominal pain and a loss of appetite, says L. R. Danny Daniel, D.V.M., a veterinarian in private practice in Covington, Louisiana.

Uterine infection. Female dogs who haven't been spayed will sometimes get a serious uterine infection called pyometra, which causes a bloody, pus-filled discharge. It usually occurs about 45 to 60 days after a dog had a heat cycle, but wasn't bred, says Dr. Daniel.

Dogs who have recently given birth can get uterine infections when part of the placenta stays behind after delivery, providing a fertile breeding ground for bacteria. This type of infection usually causes a foul-smelling vaginal discharge that starts out watery and a little red, and then gets thicker and turns dark brown and

Dogs who have recently had pups will sometimes get uterine infections that cause a genital discharge.

contains pus as the infection progresses. "You should suspect that something is wrong if the new mother, who is generally overprotective, ignores her pups or refuses to eat," says Dr. Daniel.

Miscarriage. Dogs who are pregnant will sometimes have a discharge just before they miscarry. The discharge will usually be bloody, possibly with a little pus mixed in. "This is nature's way of taking care of abnormal fetuses or an infection in the womb that would otherwise threaten the mother's life," says Dr. Daniel.

The Best Care

Get help right away. By the time a genital discharge appears, the underlying infection is probably well-advanced. "These infections can be life-threatening, so get your pet to the vet as soon as possible," says Dr. Daniel. Dogs with uterine infections will usually be given intravenous antibiotics and will stay overnight at the veterinarian's office. Infections tend to be less serious in males and will clear up within a few weeks when dogs are given oral antibiotics.

Plan ahead. Having your pet neutered will guard against almost all of the problems that can cause a genital discharge in both males and females, says Dr. Daniel. Vets recommend neutering dogs when they're about six months old.

Encourage them to drink. Dogs who get urinary tract infections usually get them more than once, so long-term prevention is important. Keeping the water bowl full of clean water will encourage dogs to drink more, which helps flush the urinary tract and prevent bacteria from multiplying, says Beverly J. Scott, D.V.M., a veterinarian in private practice in Gilbert,

Arizona. In addition, there's some evidence that cranberry juice can help prevent infections by making it more difficult for bacteria to adhere to the lining of the bladder. Most dogs don't like cranberry juice, however, so giving them lots of fresh water is usually the best choice.

 FAST FIX If you suspect that your dog has a prostate infection, it's a good idea to apply an ice pack to the penis until you can get him to the vet. This will help reduce the swelling that can be caused by a prostate infection and will make your dog more comfortable, says Dr. Daniel.

CALL FOR HELP

Veterinarians nearly always recommend spaying female dogs by the time they're six months old—not only for population control, but also to prevent infections later on. But the procedure itself can cause an infection if a little bit of the uterus is left behind. This doesn't happen very often, but when it does, you need to move quickly, to prevent the infection from getting worse.

"If your pet is listless, lacks an appetite, drinks a lot of water, and is paying a lot of attention to her backside, such as excessive licking, check under her tail for a discharge," says L. R. Danny Daniel, D.V.M., a veterinarian in private practice in Covington, Louisiana. A discharge means an infection is raging, and you'll need to get her to a veterinarian immediately, he says.

Gum Irritation

Dogs can't brush and floss their own teeth, but veterinary dentists wish they could. Gum disease is extremely common and causes problems ranging from terrible breath and tooth loss to heart disease.

The gums should be pink, glistening, and smooth. When the gums are red or swollen, it's because something is irritating the tissues.

The Usual Suspects

Periodontal disease. Irritated gums are nearly always due to periodontal disease, a condition in which bacteria in the mouth invade the gums, causing infection, swelling, and sometimes bleeding, says Taylor Wallace, D.V.M., a veterinarian in private practice in Seattle.

Healthy gums are usually pink, smooth, and firm, with no sign of inflammation or swelling.

Too much chewing. Dogs love chewing so much that they'll sometimes keep doing it even when their chews of choice are scraping and irritating the gums, says Rance Sellon, D.V.M., a veterinarian specializing in internal medicine at Washington State University in Pullman. Toys that often cause problems include rawhide and nylon chews, pig's ears, and tennis balls.

Boredom. Some dogs chew because there's nothing else to do. Dogs with excess energy will sometimes get into the habit of chewing rocks, chain-link fencing, even vinyl siding, all of which are very rough on the gums. "If you can think of it, a dog will chew on it," says Dr. Sellon.

Soft foods. The teeth get a natural brushing every time dogs eat dry, crunchy food. Those who eat only moist food, however, don't get the same teeth-cleaning and gum-massaging benefits. In addition, moist foods tend to stick to the teeth, making it easier for bacteria to flourish.

Toxins. Many of the chemicals that we use around our houses every day can be caustic. Dogs who get into such things as fish-meal fertilizer or disinfected toilet water will sometimes develop sore, irritated gums.

Internal problems. Conditions such as kidney disease and cancer can make the gums bleed. So can an immune system disorder called thrombocytopenia, which damages platelets, the cell-like structures in the blood that aid in clotting. This seems to be more of a problem in some of the small breeds, such as cocker spaniels and poodles. When the gums are bleeding and you can't figure out why, you need to get your dog to a vet for a checkup, says Dr. Sellon.

The Best Care

Use mainly dry food. Feeding dogs dry kibble rather than canned or semi-moist food will help reduce plaque, the thin, bacteria-laden film that forms on teeth and that may lead to periodontal disease or bleeding gums. Your vet may recommend giving your dog a prescription food called Hill's Science Diet Prescription Diet T/D. It's an oversize kibble that doesn't crumble at the first bite. Instead it holds together until the teeth penetrate almost all the way through. This helps wipe the teeth clean as a dog is eating.

Provide plenty of biscuits. When you're giving your dog treats, you can't do much better than to give him crunchy pet biscuits. The abrasive action of the biscuits will help keep the teeth and gums clean. Carrots, broccoli, and other raw vegetables are also good for the teeth, although most dogs won't eat them unless they're cooked—at which point they've given up most of their dental benefits.

Do a little dental care. Brushing dogs' teeth is the best way to keep the teeth and gums healthy. Rather than using a doggy toothbrush on irritated gums, moisten a gauze pad, wrap it around your finger, and rub it across the outer surfaces of the teeth and along the gumline once or twice a week, says Agnes Rupley, D.V.M., a veterinarian in private practice in College Station, Texas. Baking soda is slightly abrasive, and sprinkling some on a toothbrush or a gauze pad will get the teeth and gums even cleaner.

Some dog toothpastes contain chlorhexidine, which helps control bacteria and prevent gum infections, says Dr. Wallace. If the gums are already sore, it's better to use chlorhexidine gel, which is less abrasive than paste, she says.

Another way to help sore gums heal is to rinse the mouth with warm water, using a turkey baster, several times a day, says Dr. Wallace.

CALL FOR HELP

The average garage is filled with chemicals that can burn a dog's mouth and gums in just a few minutes. You need to call your vet immediately if your dog has gotten into fertilizer or other household chemicals. Depending on the substance, your vet may recommend taking your dog into the yard and flushing his mouth thoroughly with running water.

"Many dogs will let you spray their mouths gently with a garden hose, a kitchen sprayer, or a turkey baster," says Agnes Rupley, D.V.M., a veterinarian in private practice in College Station, Texas. Just be sure to hold his mouth so the nose is facing downward, she adds. "That way the water will flow out of his mouth instead of into his tummy."

Head-Shaking

Unlike human ears, which are smooth-skinned and open to the elements, dogs have ears that are essentially closed off. Even in breeds with perked-up ears, the combination of fur and an intricately shaped ear canal creates an environment that's warm and moist—perfect for all sorts of infections.

Dogs who are shaking or tilting their heads have some sort of problem inside the ear. It could be a burr that's stuck in too far. Or it could be an infection that's quickly getting worse.

The Usual Suspects

Outer ear infections. The most common cause of head-shaking is an infection in a part of the ear called the otis externa, or the outer ear. Caused by bacteria, yeast, or other organisms, this type of infection is especially common in dogs with large, floppy ears because the insides of their ears provide a very hospitable environment for germs, says Stephen Simpson, D.V.M., associate professor of neurology at Auburn University College of Veterinary Medicine in Auburn, Alabama.

Inner ear infections. More serious than infections of the outer ear, these occur when germs thrive and multiply somewhere inside the ear canal. This type of infection is hard to recognize simply because it occurs out of sight.

Grassy areas often contain foxtails, plants with irritating seeds that can cause a frenzy of head-shaking. Foxtails are dangerous, so call your vet for advice.

Inner ear infections may cause a discolored, smelly discharge. Some dogs will have balance problems as well.

Ear mites. These tiny parasites are rarely dangerous, but the scampering of their little feet tickles and irritates the ears, and dogs shake their heads to get relief. While cats often get ear mites, they're relatively uncommon in dogs.

Allergies. People with food allergies often get upset stomachs. Dogs with food allergies tend to get itchy. When they're not scratching their ears, they'll often shake their heads. Dogs with hay fever may also get red, swollen, and irritated ears.

Objects in the ear. Because dogs shove their heads into burrows, bushes, or anything else they're interested in, it isn't uncommon for foreign objects such as burrs or grass seeds to get into their ears. Sporting dogs who spend a lot of time outdoors, such as spaniels and

CALL FOR HELP

Dogs will sometimes shake their heads so hard that the ears essentially get whiplash, which can damage blood vessels near the surface. The resulting swelling is called an aural hematoma. Without treatment, aural hematomas can make the ear permanently disfigured, so you'll want to call your vet as soon as the swelling appears.

retrievers, have an especially high risk of getting uncomfortable things stuck in their ears.

Wounds. Unlike human ears, which are tightly attached to the head, dogs' ears can flop around quite a bit, making them vulnerable to cuts and scrapes. Dogs sometimes respond to the pain and discomfort by giving their heads a vigorous shake. Even small ear cuts can bleed quite a bit, but the bleeding usually isn't serious and will clear up within a few minutes.

Bug bites. Ticks can latch on to any part of the body, but they're particularly fond of the ears because the relatively smooth, tender skin makes it easy for them to grab on. Other pests that nibble on the ears include chiggers, spiders, and mosquitoes.

The Best Care

Check inside the ears. If you see something that doesn't belong, such as a burr or grass seed, you may have solved the problem. It's generally easy to remove small objects with your fingers, although you don't want to reach too far inside the ears or pull on anything that's firmly or deeply lodged, says Katherine Houpt, V.M.D., Ph.D., professor of physiology and director of the Animal Behavior Clinic at the College of Veterinary Medicine at Cornell University in Ithaca, New York. It's not always easy to see inside the ears, however, so you may need a small flashlight to get a better look.

Take a sniff. Ear infections, whether in the inner or outer ear, may cause a distinctive bad smell. You can usually treat outer ear infections with over-the-counter products, but infections deeper in the ear may require antibiotics. Since any infection is potentially serious, you'll want to call your vet anytime there's an odor or the ear looks red, raw, or swollen.

Get rid of mites. This is one of the easiest problems to diagnose at home. Mites leave behind a dark brown discharge that looks like coffee grounds. Pet supply

If you suspect that something is lodged inside your dog's ears, use a small flashlight to check them out.

stores sell a variety of products that will ease the itching and kill the mites. Follow the directions on the label, and your dog should start feeling better in a few days.

Before using mite medication, take a few minutes to clean the ears by flushing the canal with an ear cleaner, available from vets and pet supply stores. After squirting in the liquid, massage the base of the ears to distribute the fluid, says Craig N. Carter, D.V.M., Ph.D., head of epidemiology at the Texas Veterinary Medical Diagnostic Laboratory at Texas A&M University in College Station.

Cleaning the ears is the only way to ensure that the medication actually comes into contact with the mites, Dr. Carter explains. It's fine to clean the outer parts of the ears with a cotton ball or clean tissue, but don't use cotton swabs because they can damage the ear drum, he adds.

Keep them clean. Dogs who get ear problems once always seem to get them again, so you'll probably want to put some preventive maintenance on your calendar, says Bernadine Cruz, D.V.M., a veterinarian in private practice in Laguna Hills, California. She recommends periodically cleaning the ears with an over-the-counter ear wash or with a homemade solution consisting of three parts isopropyl alcohol to

Warmed mineral oil will help relieve an irritated ear. Squeeze in a few drops, then gently massage the base of the ear to spread the oil around.

one part white vinegar. The alcohol helps dissolve the wax and kills bacteria, and the vinegar helps prevent fungal infections, she explains.

However, alcohol can burn, so don't use this treatment when your dog is currently having a problem with cuts, sores, or irritation, she adds.

FAST FIX Veterinarians sometimes recommend treating irritated ears with a few drops of mineral oil that has been warmed to room temperature. Gently massage the base of the ear to evenly distribute the oil and loosen the wax, then swab up the excess with a cotton ball, says Tim Banker, D.V.M., a veterinarian in private practice in Greensboro, North Carolina.

BREED SPECIFIC

Schnauzers, poodles, and cocker spaniels tend to have hairy ears. Hair in the ear canal traps moisture and debris, making these dogs more likely to get infections than other breeds.

Housesoiling

Most dogs are house-trained by the time they're five months old. And once they understand the rules, they rarely break them—unless they feel they have no other choice. Well-trained dogs who are constantly having accidents in the house nearly always have a problem—one that won't disappear on its own.

The Usual Suspects

Waiting too long. Probably the most common cause of mistakes—and one that has more to do with owners than with dogs—is staying inside too long. Even dogs with excellent bowel and bladder control can't ignore Nature's call indefinitely. Most adult dogs can go as many as 10 to 12 hours between bathroom breaks—but that's really pushing their limits.

Muscle weakness. Muscles throughout the body weaken as dogs get older, and the muscles controlling the bladder and bowels are no exception. This tends to be more of a problem in older females who have been spayed because they have very little estrogen, a hormone that helps keep the muscles strong. But any older dog will probably have less control than he did when he was younger. In addition, older dogs may have arthritis or other conditions that make it difficult for them to get to the door as quickly as they should.

Infections. Dogs who are urinating in the house—not just once, but several times a day—often have a urinary tract infection, says Patrick Connolly, D.V.M., a veterinarian in private prac-

CALL FOR HELP

Finding the occasional puddle or pile doesn't make for pleasant mornings, but it doesn't necessarily represent a trend, either. Nearly every dog occasionally makes mistakes, and there's a decent chance it won't happen again—at least, for a long time.

When accidents are happening daily, or when your dog is having frequent diarrhea or is dribbling small amounts of urine, you'll want to call your veterinarian, says Patrick Connolly, D.V.M., a veterinarian in private practice in Thousand Oaks, California. Diarrhea that doesn't get better is usually a symptom of intestinal problems, and urine dribbles may mean a dog has kidney disease, Dr. Connolly explains.

tice in Thousand Oaks, California. These infections irritate the delicate tissues in the bladder or urethra, giving dogs a sense of urgency that they can't control. A similar thing happens in dogs who have the flu, Dr. Connolly adds. As with some other viral infections, flu can cause diarrhea to come on with almost no warning.

Marking territory. Dogs are instinctively driven to mark their territory so that other dogs know who it belongs to. Most dogs understand that urine-marking is only supposed to occur outside, but sometimes they feel the need to protect the inside of the house as well.

"If your dog is a domineering type and a friend brings another dog over, this might trigger housesoiling," says Dennis Fetko, Ph.D., an animal behaviorist in San Diego, California.

Territorial marking can be confusing because it doesn't necessarily happen at the same time as the original "threat", Dr. Fetko adds. Some dogs will continue to feel threatened for days, weeks, or even months, and will keep marking in order to make their presence known.

Submissive urination. When a dog wants to show another dog the ultimate form of respect, he'll roll over on his back and urinate on the spot. Among dogs, this type of behavior, called submissive urination, is usually practiced by puppies and adult dogs who are particularly shy or submissive. Dogs who do it in the human family are generally insecure about something—either because something has frightened them or because they're generally a little fearful and insecure.

"A lot of stress in the home can cause a dog who lacks confidence to lose control," says Janice DeMello, a trainer in Somis, California.

The Best Care

Let them out more often. For many dogs, going outside more often is all that's necessary to stop messes in the house, says Dr. Connolly. It's most important to let them out first thing in the morning and after meals, when the urges are strongest. You should also let them out before you go to bed because the eight to nine hours from night to morning is longer than some dogs can wait, he says. Puppies need to go outside

When another dog comes to visit, some dogs will urinate in the house to tell the intruder that this is their territory.

more often—at least every two hours during the day and every four hours at night, he adds.

Start with the basics. Dogs who are suddenly making messes often need a refresher course in basic training, says Sandy Driscoll, owner of the Academy of Dog Obedience in Los Angeles. Keep an eye on your dog whenever he is in the house. Your goal is to catch him before he lifts his leg or squats on the carpet, since it's more effective to praise good behavior when he goes in the right place than to punish him for making a mistake, she says. You don't have to

BREED SPECIFIC

Old English sheepdogs have been bred not to have tails, and veterinarians believe this genetic trait also affects their bladder control because they're more likely than other breeds to urinate where they're not supposed to.

wait until he's almost in the act before heading for the door, Driscoll adds. Letting him out more often will give him more opportunities to take care of business, and the praise you give will help him understand what he is supposed to do in the future.

Build his confidence. There's nothing wrong with dogs who urinate when they're feeling submissive around other dogs—it's a natural behavior. But it's inappropriate in human families, which is why trainers recommend looking for ways to make submissive dogs a little more confident, DeMello says.

She recommends taking a few minutes each day to run through basic obedience drills, such as practicing "sit" commands, and praising your dog when he does the right thing. Dogs who are insecure crave human approval. Teaching them simple things and rewarding their successes is the best way to bolster their confidence, she explains. When you're not practicing obedience, try taking them out in public where they'll see new places and meet new people, she adds. Dogs who urinate submissively are often afraid of all sorts of things. The more they experience, the bolder and happier they're going to be.

Make it easy for them. Older dogs may know the rules, but that's no help when their bodies aren't cooperating. You can prevent many accidents just by putting your dog's bed a bit closer to the doggy door, if there is one. If not, put his bed where you can see it. This will improve your chances of getting him outside before accidents happen.

Think about neutering. Once dogs start doing territorial marking in the house, it can be very difficult to make them stop, DeMello says. Neutering dogs, both males and females, will often stop territorial marking, especially if it's done when dogs are young. Even then, however, some dogs will always get defensive or aggressive when other dogs are around, and they may express their feelings by marking inside the house. About all you can do in these instances is leave the dogs outside or keep one or both of them in a crate, says DeMello.

ALL IN THE MIND

No matter what emotional state dogs are in, the body maintains its life-giving rhythms—to a point. Anything that causes emotional stress can cause the body's rhythms to skip a bit. And the digestive tract is especially sensitive, which is why diarrhea is one of the most common physical symptoms of emotional turmoil, says Patti Schaefer, D.V.M., a veterinarian in private practice in Olympia, Washington. Veterinarians call this condition psychogenic diarrhea. It's surprisingly common, affecting as much as 15 percent of dogs at some time in their lives.

Even small changes in a dog's usual routines, such as staying in a kennel for a weekend or spending more time than usual alone, may cause diarrhea. The stress doesn't have to be something that directly affects your dog, Dr. Schaefer adds. "Our pets can be so close to us and so in tune to us that if we are stressed, they feel it, too," she says.

Lethargy

Some dogs are slow-moving by nature, while others have nearly atomic energy. The only way to tell whether dogs are more fatigued and lethargic than usual is to know what their normal energy levels are. It's perfectly natural for a dog to be pooped after an energetic day, but lethargy that lasts more than a day or two invariably means that dogs are sick, says Sheldon A. Steinberg, V.M.D., professor of neurology at the University of Pennsylvania School of Veterinary Medicine in Philadelphia.

Lethargy that lasts for more than a few days or is accompanied by other symptoms, such as vomiting or diarrhea, should always be treated by a veterinarian. But low energy levels aren't necessarily a serious problem and can often be treated at home.

Every dog will have the occasional low-energy day, but constant lethargy can be a sign of internal problems, including anemia and thyroid disease.

The Usual Suspects

Fever. "The number one cause of lethargy is fever, usually due to an infection," says Kevin O'Neall, D.V.M., a veterinarian in private practice in Green River, Wyoming. Most fevers aren't serious and will go away when the underlying infection—often flu or a similar mild illness—clears up. A dog has a fever when his temperature rises above 102.5°F, says Dr. O'Neall.

Pain. It's usually not a problem in young dogs, but older pets sometimes develop conditions such as arthritis or hip dysplasia, which can cause long-term, fatiguing pain, says Dr.

O'Neall. A dog with joint or muscular pain is understandably reluctant to move very much, he explains. And the pain itself can make dogs feel tired and listless.

Anemia. This is a potentially serious condition in which the red blood cells aren't able to transport all the oxygen the body needs, either because there aren't enough red blood cells or because they aren't working efficiently. The lack of oxygen can make dogs feel extremely tired. In puppies, as well as small and elderly dogs, anemia may be caused by fleas or other parasites that remove blood from the body. Anemia can also be caused by ulcers or other conditions that cause internal bleeding.

Overweight. Dogs who've been spending too much time at the food bowl can accumulate a lot more weight than nature intended. This means that they have to expend more energy than they should just hauling themselves around. In addition, dogs who are overweight are often reluctant to exercise, and the lack of exercise makes them feel even more tired.

Thyroid deficiency. The thyroid gland controls the body's metabolism. Dogs who don't produce enough thyroid hormone, a condition called hypothyroidism, will be extremely listless. They'll also gain weight because the body isn't running as quickly as it should. Thyroid disease often starts when dogs are young, but symptoms may not appear until years later as the body's reserves of thyroid hormone are used up.

BREED SPECIFIC

Dogs with the highest risk of thyroid problems include boxers, Chow Chows (right), cocker spaniels, golden retrievers, Great Danes, schnauzers, and vizslas.

The Best Care

Strengthen the joints and muscles. Since joint problems are so common in older dogs, veterinarians recommend taking a few minutes each day to keep the joints loose and relaxed. You can attack joint pain in several ways.

• Rub the sore spots or apply a hot-water bottle wrapped in a towel. The combination of massage and warmth improves circulation and helps joints move with less pain.

• Joints that don't move get stiffer and more creaky. Even moderate amounts of gentle exercise increase joint lubrication and flexibility.

• Buffered or coated aspirin—the usual dose is one-quarter of a 325 milligram tablet for every 10 pounds of weight—can reduce pain and inflammation. Since aspirin may cause ulcers in some dogs, you'll want to talk to your veterinarian before using it at home.

Build the blood. Anemia sounds scary—and it is when it's not taken care of—but it's

almost always easy to treat. Pets who are losing blood because of fleas will recover their energy very quickly once the pests are gone. In addition to such things as flea shampoos, veterinarians usually recommend products such as Program and Frontline, which kill fleas and keep them from coming back, says Bernadine Cruz, D.V.M., a veterinarian in private practice in Laguna Hills, California. Worms are similarly easy to get rid of with over-the-counter and prescription medications. In addition, veterinarians often recommend giving dogs extra iron and B vitamins, which will help their red blood cells get back to normal.

Start the diet. It's easier for dogs to lose weight than it is for people, if only because they can't open the refrigerator without your help. Most dogs will readily lose weight when they eat a little less—start by giving them about 25 percent less food than they're currently getting—and exercise for about 20 minutes twice a day.

Limping

Even the fittest and most agile dogs are vulnerable to the same sorts of accidents and injuries as people. When they pull a muscle or cut their feet, they're going to limp for a few days until they heal.

The Usual Suspects

Cuts. Probably the most common cause of limping is a cut paw pad, says Grant Nisson, D.V.M., a veterinarian in private practice in West River, Maryland. Even though the pads are tough, a sharp splinter or shard of glass can puncture or slice the pad, making walking painful. Even when the pad isn't obviously injured, there may be something sharp inside, like a small splinter or grass seed. These types of puncture wounds aren't very painful unless they get infected, at which point the foot will get very tender. Bruises can also be a problem when dogs jam a foot on a stone or the edge of a stick.

Long toenails. Dogs who walk on city sidewalks have an advantage over their lawn-dwelling suburban friends because the constant friction of paws against concrete gives them natural pedicures—and short nails rarely tear or break. Dogs with long nails, however, can snag them on carpets or other rough surfaces. A torn nail can be excruciatingly painful and take a long time to heal.

Strained muscles. Dogs aren't always the most graceful creatures, and sometimes they take painful tumbles that strain muscles, tendons, or ligaments. Dogs also may get hurt when they're running at full speed, then suddenly change direction. It's not unheard of for them to tear the ligament in the knee, says Joanne Smith, D.V.M., a veterinarian in private practice in Edgewater, Maryland.

Arthritis. Limping is usually caused by injuries, but some dogs will hobble a bit when they've damaged one or more joints. Older dogs with arthritis sometimes limp. So may those with hip dysplasia, which causes wear on the hip joints and may cause a painful form of arthritis, says Susan Vargas, D.V.M., a veterinarian in private practice in Eugene, Oregon.

Tick bites. The ugliest thing about ticks isn't their bite, which most dogs never feel, but the diseases they carry. Conditions such as Lyme disease and Rocky Mountain spotted fever are transmitted by ticks and can cause sore muscles and creaky, aching joints, says Dr. Nisson.

CALL FOR HELP

Limping that doesn't start getting better within a few days should be checked by a veterinarian because it may be caused by a broken bone or a serious strain, says Bernadine Cruz, D.V.M., a veterinarian in private practice in Laguna Hills, California.

"If lameness persists for more than 48 hours, especially if it's getting worse or if there's swelling, you need to get medical attention," she says.

The Best Care

Narrow the field. To pick the best treatment, you have to work out what's making your dog limp. Vets recommend this simple check: Dogs who were fine when they went outside, but came back limping have injured themselves. However, dogs who were fine when they went to bed, but woke up with a limp may have a more serious underlying problem.

Clean the pad. Injured paw pads are probably the most common cause of limping, so it's worth taking a close look to see if there's a cut or puncture wound. Even if you're not sure, it can't hurt to clean the pad thoroughly with Betadine solution mixed with warm water. Soak the foot for 10 minutes, three times a day, and repeat for about four days, says Dr. Nisson. If the area is already infected—signs of infection include pus, swelling, or a bad smell—call your vet because your dog will probably need antibiotics, Dr. Nisson says. The same is true if there has been a deep puncture wound, since these often get infected.

Apply cold followed by heat. When you can't see anything wrong on the pad, chances are that it's bruised. Vets recommend putting ice cubes in a plastic bag wrapped in a towel and holding it against the sore spot for about 10 minutes. Repeat this three or four times during the first 24 hours. On the second day, put the ice away and apply a warm compress for 5 to 10 minutes several times a day, says Dr. Nisson. Alternating cold and hot treatments work just as well on strains and sprains, he adds.

Give a massage. Gently massaging the muscles and moving the leg through its full range of motion for about 15 minutes once or twice a

BREED SPECIFIC

Hip dysplasia is most common in large breeds, such as German shepherds, retrievers, Irish setters, and Rottweilers. Small dogs like toy poodles, however, tend to get knee injuries because their joints are small and fragile.

day will improve circulation and help strains heal more quickly, says Anna Scholey, D.V.M., a veterinarian in private practice in Dallas.

Help the body with vitamin C. This powerful antioxidant nutrient has been found to help heal tissues throughout the body, including in the joints. It seems especially effective for dogs with arthritis or hip dysplasia, says Dr. Scholey. She recommends giving small dogs about 100 milligrams of vitamin C twice a day, medium-size dogs 250 milligrams twice a day, and larger dogs 500 milligrams twice a day.

Prevent infections. You can't treat tickborne illnesses at home, but they're usually easy to prevent by running a fine-toothed comb through your pet's coat to remove ticks before they have a chance to latch on. In areas with a lot of ticks, veterinarians recommend doing this tick patrol after every walk outside.

FAST FIX When a dog is limping, Dr. Nisson recommends giving buffered or coated aspirin (such as Ascriptin). The usual dose is 10 milligrams for every pound of dog, given once or twice a day. Every dog needs different amounts, however, so check with your vet to be sure.

Lumps and Bumps

It's natural for dogs to get a little gray around their muzzles and to put on an extra pound or two when they get older. They also tend to get lumpy, as though their skin were filled with miniature water balloons.

When you don't know what's causing them, lumps and bumps should always be checked out by a veterinarian. But most lumps aren't cancer, and vets have some straightforward guidelines for knowing which lumps need attention and which can be left alone. "The most common lumps and bumps that I see are fatty tumors, cysts, and warts, which are all harmless," says Karen Zagorsky, D.V.M., a veterinarian in private practice in Moreno Valley, California.

The Usual Suspects

Fatty tumors. It's very common for older dogs to accumulate collections of fatty cells under the skin. When enough of these fatty cells clump together in one place, they form a soft, spongy lump called a lipoma. Lipomas can get to be quite large, and when you push them with your finger, they'll glide freely under the skin. Lipomas are harmless, but they can make your dog's skin feel a little like a beanbag.

Hair follicle infections. Every strand of a dog's fur is anchored in a tiny opening in the skin called a hair follicle. It's not uncommon for bacteria to multiply inside one or more follicles, causing a minor infection. The infections usually aren't any more serious—or more painful—than the pimples that people get, and most of the time they'll clear up on their own.

Hair follicle cysts. These are tiny, fluid-filled sacs that sometimes form inside hair follicles. Since the cysts are rarely larger than the end of a cotton swab, the only way you're likely to discover them is when you're brushing or petting your dog and feel a small bump.

Hair follicle cysts are rarely painful and often break open and drain on their own without causing any problems at all.

Warts. People get warts a lot more than dogs do. When dogs do get warts, called viral papillomas, they usually get them on the face or

Feeling for lumps should be a routine part of your dog's regular physical checkup.

CALL FOR HELP

With their large ears and their propensity for scratching, shaking, and otherwise banging them, dogs occasionally damage tiny blood vessels in the pinna, the flap of the ear. This can cause blood to accumulate between the ear's skin and cartilage, resulting in a tender, swollen bruise called an aural hematoma.

Aural hematomas can get to be quite large, and when they rupture, they can bleed heavily, says Lowell Ackerman, D.V.M., a veterinarian in private practice in Mesa, Arizona. The bulges can also cause permanent disfigurement or even interfere with hearing if they're not treated quickly. Once your veterinarian has drained blood and other fluids from the swelling, it will usually heal very quickly.

mouth. Warts tend to occur in young dogs, and they're easily passed from dog to dog, says Lowell Ackerman, D.V.M., a veterinary dermatologist in private practice in Mesa, Arizona. Warts range in size from about a pinhead to more than an inch across, and they're usually pinkish or gray. They look almost as though a small piece of bubble gum were stuck to your dog's skin.

The over-the-counter remedies people use for removing warts shouldn't be used on dogs because they can damage the skin. Veterinarians usually advise leaving warts alone, although sometimes—for instance, if they're interfering with eating—they'll remove them by cutting them off or freezing them with liquid nitrogen.

Sebaceous gland hyperplasia. Despite its scary-sounding name, this condition isn't likely to cause problems. It occurs when oil-producing glands in the skin grow larger or faster than they should, causing a slight bump under the skin. The overgrown glands are very common in older dogs, says Dr. Ackerman.

The Best Care

Get some advice. Since there's no way to tell at home if a lump or bump is serious or not, you'll want to call your vet as soon as you notice any changes in the skin. Hard lumps or bumps that grow quickly may be serious. You should also be suspicious of lumps that appear to be growing from a bone or from inside the breast or a nipple.

"While the majority of skin lumps are harmless, many cancers are indistinguishable from benign cysts and tumors," says Lillian Roberts, D.V.M., a veterinarian in private practice in Palm Desert, California.

Treat the infection. Lumps caused by skin infections are usually easy to recognize because there may be pus, or the area will be warm, red, and tender. Applying a warm, moist compress several times a day for five minutes at a time will help the infection drain. After applying the compress, dry the area well, then apply an over-the-counter triple antibiotic ointment.

Leave them alone. Since most lumps and bumps aren't painful or harmful, veterinarians usually recommend leaving them alone once they've made sure they're not cancer. In the rare cases when lumps are painful, they're usually easy to remove.

Nail Changes

Unlike humans, whose nails are good for trapping dirt and not much else, dogs use their nails all the time for digging and scratching. And since the nails are always touching the ground, they come into contact with a lot of hard, rough surfaces. So the nails take quite a beating, and sometimes they crack or splinter. Cracked nails are not only painful but also they're prone to hard-to-treat infections, which can cause even more cracking.

The Usual Suspects

Long nails. Nails that are short rarely get damaged, but nails that are allowed to get too long get weaker and are more prone to cracks or tears, says Lila Miller, D.V.M., senior director of animal sciences and veterinary adviser to the American Society for the Prevention of Cruelty to Animals in New York City.

This is often a problem with the dew claw on the inner side of the foot because it doesn't get worn down from touching the ground. In addition, long nails are hooked, making it easy for them to get caught in carpeting and tear.

Infections. Because dogs don't wear shoes, their feet are constantly exposed to the environment and all the bacteria that it contains. Dogs who spend a lot of their time in water or moist conditions have a higher risk of getting nail infections because many organisms thrive in the presence of moisture.

Lack of fatty acids. Though they don't look or feel like skin, nails are really an extension of

Bacteria thrive in moist conditions, so dogs who spend time in or around water have a higher chance than others of getting nail infections.

the skin layer. Anything that causes unhealthy skin, such as a lack of necessary fats in the diet, can cause nails to crack, says Nancy E. Wiswall, D.V.M., a veterinarian in private practice in Bethesda, Maryland.

Twenty-nail disease. It's not very common, but dogs sometimes develop a condition called lupoid onchyodystrophy, or 20-nail disease, in which all of the nails fall out. When they grow back, they will usually be brittle and prone to cracking, says Grant Nisson, D.V.M., a veterinarian in private practice in West River, Maryland. Veterinarians aren't sure what causes this condition, although it may be related to the immune system, he says.

HOW TO TRIM NAILS

Unless your pet has an underlying illness, keeping the nails trimmed will usually prevent them from cracking. Most pets' nails need trimming about once a month, although older dogs may need more frequent pedicures, says Nancy E. Wiswall, D.V.M., a veterinarian in private practice in Bethesda, Maryland.

- Cracked nails tend to splinter during trimming, so use a sharp trimmer—either a side-to-side-style trimmer designed for thick nails, or simply a nail file to slowly work the nails back. Don't use guillotine-style trimmers because they tend to crush brittle nails.

- Before starting, soak the nails for 15 minutes in warm water to make them easier to cut, suggests Dr. Wiswall.

- If your dog won't sit still for soaking, dip a cloth in warm water and wrap it around the foot for 10 to 15 minutes. If you don't want to hold the foot for that long, cover the cloth with a plastic bag and tape it on.

- Some dogs hate having their nails trimmed, so you'll probably have to clip one or two nails, wait a day or two, and then clip

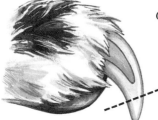

Cut only the tips of the nails, to avoid damaging the sensitive quick.

a couple more, advises Tim Banker, D.V.M., a veterinarian in private practice in Greensboro, North Carolina.

- When trimming nails, be careful not to cut into the quick, the inner part of a nail that contains nerves and blood vessels. Many dogs have black nails, so the quick is hard to see. All you can really do is trim away tiny parts of the nail at a time, stopping when it starts getting a little softer. If you do cut into the quick, stop the bleeding by dabbing with a styptic pen or dusting with flour or cornstarch.

- "You can start trimming a puppy's nails as early as 10 to 12 weeks of age," says Lila Miller, D.V.M., senior director of animal sciences and veterinary adviser of the American Society for the Prevention of Cruelty to Animals in New York City. At that age it's best to clip only the sharp tips, allowing puppies to get used to having their feet handled.

Using sharp clippers, snip away the tip of the nail. Avoid using guillotine clippers on cracked nails; use the side-by-side style instead.

CALL FOR HELP

Infections that occur in the nails or the nail beds can be serious because they're time-consuming and difficult to treat. If your dog is suddenly limping or favoring one foot, take a look at the nails. Nail infections usually have pus or a black, gummy discharge, and you'll want to call your vet right away.

Even when you catch them early, nail infections can take quite a long time to heal. Some dogs will need to take antibiotics for at least a month.

Even with fast treatment, some nail infections simply won't heal. If that happens, your veterinarian may recommend removing the nails. It's not a difficult or dangerous procedure, but it does require general anesthetic and a day in the hospital. If your vet only removes the dead portion of the nail, it will gradually grow back. In some cases, however, it is necessary to remove the entire nail, in which case it won't come back.

The Best Care

Try a better food. If you've been using a cut-rate food, you may want to switch to a better-quality, name-brand food, which will probably contain more fatty acids. In addition, your vet may recommend giving your dog dietary supplements containing fatty acids, available in health food and pet supply stores. Every dog needs different amounts, so ask your vet for the correct dose.

Dietary changes are often helpful, but they don't work quickly, says Dr. Wiswall. It can take more than six months for a nail to grow out tougher and stronger than it was originally.

Keep the feet dry. To reduce the risk of infections, it's important to make sure that dogs don't spend a lot of time on wet or muddy ground, says Anna Scholey, D.V.M., a veterinarian in private practice in Dallas. Dogs who stay outdoors in a kennel or run will usually have healthier feet if the ground is concrete rather than dirt, possibly with clean shavings in one part so they can relax in comfort.

For working dogs, who can't always avoid wet surroundings, or for those who just can't resist playing in water, drying their feet as often as is practicable will help keep infections at bay.

Wet feet are an invitation to infections, so keeping them dry will help keep the nails healthy.

Nose-Color Changes

Some dogs will occasionally lose pigment from their noses, causing them to turn white or red. This is rarely a health problem, but it looks unusual, to say the least. And for folks who show their pets, a fading nose can keep a dog out of competition until the normal color returns—if, in fact, it ever does.

The Usual Suspects

Allergies. "The first thing that I ask people whose dogs have a nose discoloration problem is whether they serve pets their food in plastic dishes," says John Hamil, D.V.M., a veterinarian in private practice in Laguna Beach, California. Some dogs are sensitive to plastic, he explains. Putting their noses in plastic feeding dishes every day may eventually cause the pigments in the nose skin to fade.

Irritation. Scrapes or cuts on the nose will often cause color changes, at least for a while. "The pigment will migrate out of the area, and then after the nose heals, the pigment will slowly migrate back," says Dr. Hamil.

Internal illnesses. It hasn't been proven, but some veterinarians believe that low thyroid levels may cause the nose to lose its color.

In addition, immune-system diseases such as lupus and pemphigus can cause the nose to fade. Another immune disorder, called Harada's syndrome, damages the eyes as well as the pigment in the skin. Veterinarians often treat this condition with steroids, which help keep the immune system under control.

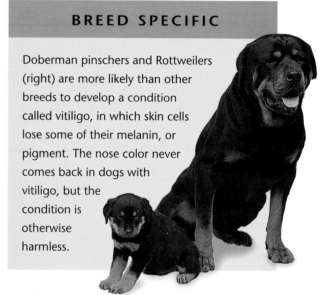

BREED SPECIFIC

Doberman pinschers and Rottweilers (right) are more likely than other breeds to develop a condition called vitiligo, in which skin cells lose some of their melanin, or pigment. The nose color never comes back in dogs with vitiligo, but the condition is otherwise harmless.

Snow nose. Veterinarians aren't sure why, but many breeds of dogs—particularly collie types and Nordic breeds such as Siberian huskies, American Eskimo dogs, and Alaskan malamutes—will lose pigment from their noses during the winter months. Veterinarians once thought that this condition, called snow nose, was caused by bright sunlight reflecting off snow and bleaching the nose white, or by a combination of cold and trauma, since dogs often use their noses as miniature snow shovels. Vets have found, however, that even dogs living in warm climates may get snow nose, so weather doesn't appear to be a factor.

Sunlight. Most of a dog's body is covered by fur, or at least tough skin. The nose, however, is hairless and tender and easily becomes sunburned, causing it either to lighten or to darken.

Call for Help

The nose is packed with capillaries—small blood vessels that normally carry bright red blood. A dog whose nose suddenly takes on a bluish cast could be developing cyanosis, a condition in which the blood isn't carrying enough oxygen. Cyanosis is a sign of breathing problems that may be caused by a heart condition, says Peggy Rucker, D.V.M., a veterinarian in private practice in Lebanon, Virginia. "We see this a lot in Pomeranians," she says. "Their owners notice the strange change in the color of their dog's nose long before they pick up on the fact that the dog is breathing hard."

Cyanosis is always an emergency that requires a veterinarian's care. But nose color can't always be the giveaway clue because you can't see the bluish tint in dogs with dark-colored noses, Dr. Rucker adds.

The Best Care

Switch to glass, ceramic, or metal bowls. Plastic allergies aren't all that common, but they happen often enough that many veterinarians routinely advise using hypoallergenic feeding bowls made of metal, glass, or ceramic. If an allergy to plastic is causing the nose changes, you'll probably start to see improvements within a few weeks.

Give supplements a try. Some breeders swear that giving dogs vitamin E and kelp, available in health food stores, will help restore the color in dogs who have snow nose. There's no evidence that it works, but the supplements are safe and are certainly worth a try. Ask your veterinarian to recommend the right dose for your dog.

Protect against sunlight. While most dogs can spend hours in the sun without any problem, those whose noses have faded, or those with white, tan, or red coats, will benefit from a little protection. Peggy Rucker, D.V.M., a veterinarian in private practice in Lebanon, Virginia, recommends slathering their noses with sunscreen with a sun protection factor (SPF) of at least 15. Dogs invariably lick it off, so you'll have to reapply it often. Be sure to use a screen that doesn't contain zinc oxide or PABA, which can be harmful when taken internally, she adds.

Nose-color changes caused by sunburn are very similar to changes caused by lupus or pemphigus, she adds, so call your vet if the nose has not regained its color in about two weeks.

Some dogs lose the pigment in their noses because of an allergy to the plastic in their bowls. Feeding them out of metal, glass, or ceramic bowls will solve the problem.

Nose Discharge

Dogs don't get drippy noses as often as people do because much of their histamine—the body chemical that's often responsible for nasal discharges—is concentrated in the skin rather than in the nasal passages. When their noses do run, the best thing you can do is check the color of the discharge. That will tell you a lot about what's causing the problem and whether you can treat it at home.

The Usual Suspects

Viral infections. It's not uncommon for dogs to get mild viral infections, and these will often cause a clear nasal discharge, says John Angus, D.V.M., a veterinarian in private practice in Mesa, Arizona. Most viral infections will clear up on their own in a few days. In the meantime, however, your dog could be contagious and infect other dogs, says Dr. Angus.

Bacterial and fungal infections. While viral respiratory infections usually aren't serious, those caused by bacteria or fungi can be a real problem because they'll usually get worse unless dogs are treated with medications, says Dr. Angus. "If the discharge is bloody, thick, milky, or green, it's time to visit your veterinarian," he advises.

Allergies. Dogs with allergies are more likely to be itchy than sniffly, but occasionally, their noses will start running, too. Any allergy can cause a nasal discharge, but usually it's an inhalant allergy—one that's caused by breathing airborne pollen, molds, or dust, says Lowell

Dogs with allergies such as hay fever usually get itchy skin, but sometimes their noses start running as well.

Ackerman, D.V.M., a veterinary dermatologist in private practice in Mesa, Arizona. As with discharges caused by viral infections, an allergy-related discharge is usually clear and watery, Dr. Ackerman adds.

Obstructions. A dog's nose can generate enough suction power to sniff up twigs and even small stones. Once something gets lodged in the nose, it can cause a copious, clear discharge. Dogs can usually dislodge objects by sneezing or shaking their heads. Objects that stay inside, however, will irritate the nasal passages and possibly cause an infection.

Broken blood vessels. The blood vessels that line the nasal passages are very small and delicate, and an energetic sneeze or two will sometimes cause them to break. A nasal discharge that's tinged with blood usually isn't serious as long as it goes away in a day or two. If it doesn't, you'll want to call your vet, because there could be substantial nasal damage—or something more serious, such as a tumor—that's causing the bleeding.

The Best Care

Protect the nose. Most nasal discharges aren't serious, but the persistent dripping can irritate the delicate skin on the nose, says James Tilley, D.V.M., a veterinarian in private practice in Prescott, Arizona. He recommends wiping the nose periodically with a warm, damp cloth, and then applying a human moisturizer to keep the skin lubricated. Most dogs, of course, will lick off the moisturizer within a few seconds, so you'll want to distract your dog or keep him busy until it has had time to soak in.

CALL FOR HELP

Distemper isn't very common anymore thanks to vaccinations, but dogs who get this dangerous viral infection will be extremely ill and in some cases may not recover. An early warning signs of distemper is a crusty, grayish yellow discharge on the nose and at the corners of the eyes. Call your vet right away if you notice this type of discharge—or any time a discharge is thick or discolored.

Stop allergy symptoms. Vets often recommend treating allergies with over-the-counter antihistamines, such as Benadryl, says Dr. Ackerman. Antihistamines work fairly quickly and are safe for dogs to take throughout the allergy season. The usual dose is one to three milligrams for every pound of dog, although you'll want to ask your vet for the precise amount.

Do a nose check. A quick way to tell if something is blocking one of the nasal passages is to hold a small mirror under the nostrils. If it mists on one side and not the other, you can be pretty sure there's something in there. Most nasal obstructions are near the outside and you may be able to see something if you light the nostrils with a flashlight and look inside. You can try to remove objects with blunt-tipped tweezers, but most dogs won't hold still, and you may wind up poking where you didn't mean to. Regardless of what's in there, your vet will probably be able to remove it in a few seconds.

BREED SPECIFIC

Collies (right) and pugs don't necessarily get stuffy noses more than other dogs, but because of the shapes of their noses—long and narrow in the one case and short and squashed in the other—even small amounts of congestion can make them very uncomfortable.

Pad Cracks

The paw pads are covered with thick, resilient skin that acts as shock absorbers every time the feet hit the ground. The pads are designed to last a lifetime, but in dogs who do a lot of running on hard surfaces, the skin can thicken, forming a hard callus. Calluses are tough, but they aren't very flexible and they easily dry out, causing painful cracks.

Most pad cracks are caused by wear and tear, but they may be caused by a variety of internal problems as well, says John Angus, D.V.M., a veterinarian in private practice in Mesa, Arizona.

The Usual Suspects

Allergies. Hay fever and sometimes food allergies can make the feet intensely itchy. Dogs respond by biting and licking their feet, and the friction and perpetual dampness can weaken the skin, making the pads raw and sore. As the skin weakens, cracks begin to form.

Zinc deficiency. Arctic breeds, such as American Eskimo dogs, Siberian huskies, and Alaskan malamutes, have trouble getting all the zinc they need in their diets, says Lowell Ackerman, D.V.M., a veterinary dermatologist in private practice in Mesa, Arizona. The skin needs zinc to rebuild itself, and when zinc levels fall, the paw pads may start cracking, he says.

Immune system problems. Autoimmune disorders such as lupus may cause the body to begin attacking the skin, causing painful cracks. These illnesses can come on fairly quickly, so

if your dog is suddenly developing pad cracks even when he hasn't been active, you'll want to get him in for a checkup, says Dr. Ackerman.

The Best Care

Moisturize the pads. Most pad cracks occur when the skin is hard and brittle. Applying a moisturizer once or twice a day for a few weeks will lubricate the skin, helping cracks heal and preventing new ones from forming, says John Daugherty, D.V.M., a veterinarian in private practice in Poland, Ohio. Any moisturizer will help, but veterinarians usually recommend a product called Kerasolv. Available from veterinarians, it helps keep the skin soft and supple.

It takes time for the moisturizer to soak in, so you'll probably want to put your dog's feet in socks to keep him from licking the moisturizer. Dr. Daugherty recommends putting cotton balls

Applying moisturizer to cracked paw pads will soothe the soreness and help them heal.

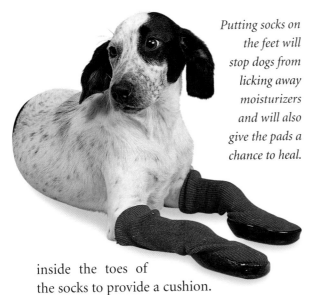

Putting socks on the feet will stop dogs from licking away moisturizers and will also give the pads a chance to heal.

inside the toes of the socks to provide a cushion. Tape the socks in place, being careful not to make the tape so tight that it restricts circulation.

Invest in some boots. "For severe cracking, protective boots can be placed on the feet to allow them to heal," says Dr. Daugherty. Pet supply stores and catalogs sell a variety of boots in different sizes. A lot of dogs won't wear boots, however, and will pull and chew at them the whole time. Socks are usually a more acceptable—and affordable—remedy.

Stop the itching. Since allergies are a very common cause of itchy feet, you'll want to talk to your vet about finding out what exactly your dog is allergic to. It's never easy to know for sure because so many things, from mold spores and pollen to ingredients in food, may cause itchy feet, says Dr. Ackerman. You may need to see a veterinarian who specializes in allergies to find out what the problem is.

In the meantime, many vets recommend giving dogs over-the-counter antihistamines such as diphenhydramine (Benadryl). The usual dose is one to three milligrams for every pound of dog, but you'll want to ask your vet for the precise dose. Antihistamines work quickly and will usually stop itching within a few days.

Clean the pads thoroughly. Dogs don't walk in the cleanest places, and pad cracks make it easy for bacteria to get inside. To prevent infections, veterinarians recommend soaking the pads in a solution made from a tablespoon of 2 percent chlorhexidine (available from drugstores) mixed into two quarts of cool water. Soak the foot for 15 minutes twice a day. If your dog won't stand still with his foot in a bucket, soak a cloth in the solution and press it gently on the pad for about 10 minutes twice a day.

Give them some time off. Pad cracks are often slow to heal because of the pressure and friction caused by walking. Dogs won't stay in bed watching television, but you can reduce paw stress by walking them only on grass or other soft surfaces until the feet heal.

INJURY OR ILLNESS?

Most pad cracks are caused by a combination of skin dryness and normal wear-and-tear—from scuffing the pads on concrete or other rough surfaces, for example. One way to tell what's causing the cracks is to see whether they're appearing on all four feet. A crack on one foot usually means there's been an injury of some sort. Cracks on all four feet may be a sign of internal problems.

Panting

Dogs have a few sweat glands on the bottoms of their feet, but that's hardly enough to keep them cool in hot weather. Apart from submerging themselves in water or digging a burrow in a patch of cool dirt, their only way of staying cool is to pant.

"If they weren't able to pant they would simply collapse from the heat," says C. Dave Richards, D.V.M., a veterinarian in private practice in Valdosta, Georgia.

After exercise or on a hot day, it's normal for dogs to pant a lot. But when they're panting even on cool days or when they're calm and relaxed, something is happening that's making them feel warmer than usual, explains John Daugherty, D.V.M., a veterinarian in private practice in Poland, Ohio.

Dogs who love water won't think twice about cooling themselves down in a handy stream or pond.

The Usual Suspects

Anxiety. If you want to see a lot of dogs panting all at once, look around the waiting room at your veterinarian's office. Just as people breathe a little faster when they're nervous, dogs start panting and keep it up until they can relax.

Anemia. Most often caused by blood loss—because of a bad case of fleas or other parasites, for example—anemia is a condition in which red blood cells are either in short supply or they aren't carrying enough oxygen. Dogs with anemia will breath more quickly in order to accelerate the rate at which oxygen enters the blood and travels to the body's cells.

Fever. A dog's normal temperature is between 99.5°F and 102.5°F. Dogs who are hotter than this pant to dispel the excess heat. Fevers are rarely dangerous and will go away when the underlying illness does, although a fever over 103°F is getting high and you'll want to call your vet, says Karen Mateyak, D.V.M., a veterinarian in private practice in Brooklyn, New York.

Thyroid disease. The thyroid gland has been called the body's gas pedal. It regulates the speed at which the metabolism operates. Dogs that produce too much thyroid hormone, a condition called hyperthyroidism, are on permanent full-throttle, and they'll pant to cool down.

The Best Care

Lower the fever. Dogs with viral infections or other illnesses will often run a fever for

Dipping a towel in cool water, wringing it out, and then applying it to your dog's stomach will help relieve high temperatures that cause panting.

result in considerable blood loss. If your dog has started panting a lot and you also see flea "dirt" on the belly—or live fleas in his coat or on the carpet—ask your veterinarian about the latest flea-control medications. Or wash your dog with an anti-flea shampoo, followed by a spritz of a pyrethrin-based flea product, available at pet supply stores.

several days, making them feel hot and miserable. Give nature a hand by applying a cool, moist towel to your dog's belly several times a day, says Dr. Mateyak. Dogs who like the water will cool off even more quickly when they're encouraged to lie in a cool tub or a wading pool for a few minutes. You don't want them to get cold, just to take the edge off their heat, she says.

Do the gum test. Most dogs have gums that are bubble-gum pink. Dogs with anemia usually have gums that are pale or even white because there isn't enough blood to give them their usual color, says Knox Inman, D.V.M., a veterinarian in private practice in West River, Maryland. If you're not sure what color the gums usually are, here's another test: Press on the gums with your finger. The spot should turn pale, then quickly return to pink. In dogs with anemia, the gums stay pale for several seconds.

Get rid of parasites. Fleas can remove a surprising amount of blood very quickly. In puppies especially, an infestation of fleas can

CALL FOR HELP

Apart from internal illnesses such as thyroid disease, one of the most common—and dangerous—conditions that cause heavy panting is heatstroke, in which the internal temperature can suddenly shoot above 104°F. Leaving dogs in the car on hot days, even for short periods, is a common cause of heatstroke. Dogs with heatstroke will pant heavily and will be extremely exhausted. Other symptoms include drooling, glassy eyes, and deep red gums.

Heatstroke is an emergency, and you'll need to get your dog to a veterinarian immediately, says John Daugherty, D.V.M., a veterinarian in private practice in Poland, Ohio. If you can't, try to lower your dog's temperature by covering him with wet towels, then wrapping him with plastic trash bags filled with ice. Or put him in a cool bath and hold a cool compress on his head.

Take his temperature every 5 to 10 minutes. Once it cools to 103°F, you can stop the treatments and let him rest until you can get him to a vet, says Dr. Daugherty.

Scooting on Bottom

You'll occasionally see dogs suddenly stop, bend their back legs, and begin dragging their bottoms across the ground. Then they stand up and take a few steps—and drop to the ground again.

Scooting is a silly sight, but it serves a very practical purpose. "Most often, a pet who is scooting along on his bottom is trying to relieve an itch," says Terri McGinnis, D.V.M., a veterinarian in private practice in the San Francisco area and author of *The Well Dog Book*.

The Usual Suspects

Blocked anal sacs. On either side of the anus, inside the body and out of sight, are two little sacs that contain a strong-smelling fluid. This fluid—which is unique to each dog, just as fingerprints are to each human—is released every time dogs have bowel movements. (Dogs sniff each others' bottoms in order to smell the fluid, which gives them vital information about each other's sex, age, and health.)

However, when the tiny opening leading from one or both of the sacs gets blocked—either because the openings are naturally small or because an infection has made the fluid thicker than usual—the fluid can't get out and the sacs swell, making them itchy and uncomfortable, says Dr. McGinnis. Older, less active dogs tend to have more anal sac problems than younger dogs because they have less muscle tone around the rectum, which means the sacs are less likely to empty on their own.

Worms. Dogs get worms often, especially when they spend a lot of time outside where other dogs have been. Tapeworms are a common cause of scooting. They live in the intestines of infected dogs, but sometimes they migrate to the anal area and irritate the skin. Tapeworms are easy to spot—just lift your dog's tail, says Lori A. Wise, D.V.M., a veterinarian in private practice in Wheat Ridge, Colorado. Tapeworms resemble grains of white rice, and they'll either be on the skin around the anus or in the fur nearby. There will also be worm segments in your dog's stools.

CALL FOR HELP

Blocked anal sacs are uncomfortable, but they rarely cause serious problems. The exception is when one or both of the sacs gets infected. This can lead to a painful and potentially dangerous abscess. If the anal area looks red or swollen, or if there's pus or your dog is crying while scooting across the ground, you'll want to get him to a veterinarian right away.

Anal sacs don't get infected all that often, however. Most of the time they just need to be emptied, which will relieve the pressure inside and stop the scooting. It's possible for you to empty anal sacs in just a few seconds, if you have a strong stomach and are willing to give it a try. Most people prefer to have their veterinarians do it instead.

Irritation. Dogs aren't very careful about what they eat and will happily chomp bones or sticks to smithereens. While these fragments pass easily enough through the intestines, they sometimes get lodged in the rectum, the last section of the large intestine. Dogs will scoot in order to relieve the irritation, says Dan Carey, D.V.M., a veterinarian with the Iams pet food company in Dayton, Ohio.

The irritation usually clears up fairly quickly unless something large is stuck inside the rectum. If you see something stuck where it shouldn't be, don't try to remove it yourself because you could damage the delicate tissues, Dr. Carey says. You'll want to call your vet for advice.

The Best Care

Get rid of the worms. Tapeworms are an extremely common parasite. Even though it's easy to get rid of them with medications, available from veterinarians and pet supply stores, they often come back because there are so many places they can hide.

Cleaning stools from the yard every day will help prevent dogs from getting reinfected, says Dr. Wise. In addition, dogs who spend time outdoors need to be discouraged from scavenging or hunting because birds and rodents often harbor tapeworms.

Get rid of fleas. Most dogs get tapeworms from fleas, which often carry immature forms of the worms. Getting rid of fleas will usually elim-

Most dogs love chewing sticks, but any sharp bits that they swallow may get stuck in the rectum and cause irritation. Dogs will scoot to ease the pain.

inate the worms as well, says Lila Miller, D.V.M., senior director of animal sciences and veterinary adviser of the American Society for the Prevention of Cruelty to Animals in New York City.

Until recently, the only treatment for fleas was to wash dogs with medicated shampoos or to spray or powder them with insecticides. Most veterinarians now recommend getting rid of fleas with oral medications such as Program or with topical liquids such as Frontline. These products are safe for dogs and will either kill fleas outright or disrupt their life cycles and so stop them from multiplying.

Scratching, Chewing, or Licking

It seems as though dogs are always scratching. Veterinarians aren't sure what makes dogs so itchy, although their skin appears to be unusually sensitive. Things that don't bother people very much, like the occasional bug bite, can send dogs' hind legs into perpetual motion.

A little scratching is fine, but some dogs aren't able to quit. The skin can only take so much abuse before it starts getting sore, irritated, and sometimes infected.

The Usual Suspects

Fleas. Many dogs are allergic to fleas—a condition that vets call flea-allergy dermatitis. When fleas bite, they inject a little saliva under the skin, says Bill Martin, D.V.M., a veterinarian in private practice in Fletcher, North Carolina.

BREED SPECIFIC

Dogs with light-colored coats and pale skin, such as blond cocker spaniels and West Highland white terriers (left), have a higher risk of skin problems than those with darker complexions. Irish setters are also very prone to skin allergies.

This can result in a flood of histamine, a chemical that causes itching, runny eyes, and other allergy symptoms. It doesn't take many bites to set off this reaction. In dogs with flea allergies, just one bite can trigger a week's worth of scratching.

Flea allergies usually flare in late spring and summer, when fleas are at their worst. But once dogs start scratching, they often get itchier and itchier, even when the fleas themselves are gone.

Fleas are easiest to see on the belly, where the fur is thin. In addition, dogs with fleas usually have telltale dark specks in their coats, which are the waste that fleas leave behind. The scratching caused by fleas is usually concentrated on a dog's back half, mainly around the rump near the base of the tail.

Mites. Another cause of scratching is the sarcoptic mite, or scabies. These mites are highly contagious and readily passed from dog to dog. Along with itching, dogs with mites often have other symptoms, such as reddened, crusty areas of skin and possibly patches of baldness. They tend to be itchiest on the chest, abdomen, legs, and the edges of the ears. You can buy mite medications at pet supply stores.

Allergies. Dogs with allergies usually have skin reactions. There are literally hundreds of things dogs may be allergic to, but they tend to fall into three main groups.

• Food allergies usually occur when dogs have a reaction to one or more of the proteins in their diets. (Occasionally, allergies are caused by food additives such as dyes or preservatives.) Protein sources such as beef, pork, soy, and corn are common causes of allergies. Veterinarians aren't sure why, but even dogs who have been eating the same food for years may suddenly develop an allergy to one of the ingredients.

• Inhalant allergies such as hay fever occur when dogs breathe in substances that they happen to be allergic to, such as pollen, dust, or mold. Inhalant allergies often occur seasonally, which means that the itching is likely to be worse in the spring and summer than in the cold months. Dogs who are allergic to dust, however, may be itchy all year long. A severe form of hay fever, called atopy, may occur in dogs who are unusually sensitive to pollens or other airborne particles. Atopy is an extremely itchy condition, causing pets to scratch at their faces and armpits and to lick and bite their feet.

• Contact allergies occur when dogs become overly sensitive to things they come in contact with. Some dogs have skin reactions when they roll on grass. Others are sensitive to chemicals in rug cleaners. Others still are allergic to nylon fibers found in many carpets.

The Best Care

Get rid of fleas. Fleas are hard to get rid of for the simple reason that they are incredibly prolific. A few fleas can produce hundreds of thousands of offspring within a few months. What's more, for every flea that you see on your dog, there may be hundreds more in the yard, on the carpets, and in his bedding. To get rid of fleas, you have to hit them everywhere they live.

Most veterinarians recommend using medications such as Frontline or Advantage, which either kill fleas directly or stop the eggs from maturing, says Bernadine Cruz, D.V.M., a veterinarian in private practice in Laguna Hills, California. If you don't want to use medications, you can get rid of most fleas by washing dogs with a flea shampoo, which will send most of the fleas down the drain. This only works if you clean and vacuum your house thoroughly. If you don't, fleas in various stages of development in the carpets and under baseboards will quickly climb on board.

Many dogs are allergic to grass. They'll roll to relieve the itch, and if they happen to roll on grass, the itching will keep getting worse.

Protect the skin. If you suspect that your dog is allergic to something he's coming into contact with, but you're not sure what it is, you can give short-term protection by using a protective cream. Rubbing the skin with an aloe-vera based hand cream, for example, will put a protective layer between your dog and whatever he's been reacting to, says Dr. Martin. Calamine lotion also works, although it's messy to apply.

Limit what he breathes. It's very difficult to protect dogs from hay fever because particles of mold, pollen, and dust are nearly impossible to avoid. About all you can do is keep your dog indoors as much as possible during the allergy season, or at least during the windiest times of day, says Dr. Cruz. "Installing an air filter will help keep the dust and pollen out of the air," she adds. Some veterinarians recommend giving antihistamines such as Benadryl to dogs with hay fever. Every dog needs a different dose, however, so check with your vet before giving antihistamines at home.

Look into food allergies. Of all the allergies that cause skin irritations, food allergies are among the hardest to identify because commercial foods contain so many ingredients that it's difficult to know which one is responsible. Your veterinarian may recommend putting your dog on an elimination diet, in which he's temporarily given a food that contains none of the ingredients that are in his usual food. If his itching and scratching go away, you can be pretty sure that he has food allergies.

The next step, says Dr. Cruz, is to gradually reintroduce the ingredients, one at a time, to see which one will set off your dog's itching and scratching again. Once you know that, you can

CALL FOR HELP

Once dogs get in the habit of scratching, chewing, or licking their skin, it can be difficult to make them stop. The constant moisture and friction can damage the skin, making dogs vulnerable to painful and hard-to-treat infections, says Bill Martin, D.V.M., a veterinarian in private practice in Fletcher, North Carolina.

"Have your dog checked early before the scratching and chewing get out of hand," he says. Scratching for a few minutes each day is probably normal. Scratching that seems more intense than usual and lasts more than five to six days needs professional care.

relieve his symptoms by buying foods that don't contain the problem ingredient.

Elimination diets can take months in some cases, so you'll want to work with your veterinarian to make sure that your dog's nutrition stays up to par during the testing time.

FAST FIX The quickest way to stop scratching is to douse dogs with Burrow's solution, available in grocery stores and drugstores, says Dr. Martin. Mix a packet of the crystals in a quart of water. Soak a cotton ball in the solution and dab the irritated spots for five minutes once or twice a day. For a more thorough drenching, plug your bathtub and pour the solution over your dog while he's standing in it. Then scoop up the liquid that runs off, repeating the process several times.

Seizures

The remarkable thing about seizures is that dogs don't feel any discomfort at all. Whether the seizure only causes a mild tremor and a little confusion or results in a full-blown, violent attack, dogs are essentially unconscious the whole time. "Watching a seizure is harder for you than it is for them," says Agnes Rupley, D.V.M., a veterinarian in private practice in College Station, Texas. "They're completely unaware that it's happening."

Seizures are caused by a flash of abnormal electrical activity in the brain. They're unlikely to cause serious harm as long as they don't last too long. In many cases, in fact, a dog could be having a seizure right in front of you and you wouldn't know that it was happening. Whether seizures are big or small, however, the underlying conditions that may be causing them are potentially quite serious.

The Usual Suspects

Epilepsy. In dogs less than four years old, seizures are generally caused by a condition called idiopathic epilepsy, which means seizures that don't have a known cause, says Mike Herrington, D.V.M., a veterinary neurologist in private practice in Redmond, Washington.

"When the first seizure is after four years of age, then infection, inflammation, or tumors are more likely to blame," says Dr. Herrington.

Low blood sugar. Dogs who are young, thin, or small sometimes have low levels of blood sugar, which can trigger seizures, says Taylor Wallace, D.V.M., a veterinarian in private practice in Seattle. "Even big, beefy hunting dogs can have seizures from low blood sugar after prolonged, intense activity," she adds.

Low calcium levels. Dogs who are nursing a litter will sometimes have very low calcium levels because their puppies are draining their calcium reserves. Low levels of calcium can sometimes trigger seizures, says Dr. Wallace.

Poisoning. Dogs who have been exposed to poisons—anything from snail, slug, or rodent bait to excessive amounts of flea or tick dips—will sometimes have seizures. And any kind of accident that damages the

Dogs love to explore open cupboards, but some household cleaners and chemicals can cause seizures if dogs eat them.

brain can also cause seizures. Some dogs will have seizures for a few days or weeks after an accident, and then never have another one. Others will continue to have seizures for the rest of their lives.

The Best Care

Watch and wait. Once a seizure has begun, about all you can do is stand by to make sure your dog doesn't collapse onto things or fall down a flight of stairs.

"A dog who's having a seizure is no danger to himself, but his environment can hurt him," says Dr. Herrington, who recommends moving quickly to clear some space so your dog doesn't bump into things or knock lamps or other objects over onto himself. "If he is near a deck or stairs, try to block his path by standing in the way," Dr. Herrington says.

Keep your hands clear. When dogs are in the midst of a seizure, they'll sometimes gnash their teeth or lash out with their legs, says Dr. Herrington. It doesn't do any good to try to restrain them or pick them up, and you could get hurt, he warns.

CALL FOR HELP

Even people who are conscientious about keeping their dog out of the garage or other places where poisons are kept may forget about one of the most dangerous toxins of all: lead. Lead poisoning can cause seizures even in very healthy dogs, says Taylor Wallace, D.V.M., a veterinarian in private practice in Seattle. "Because dogs will chew anything, you need to recognize potential sources of lead poisoning, including vinyl flooring, fishing sinkers, caulking, carpet padding, paint, and golf balls," she says.

Ask about diet. Dogs with blood sugar problems may be less likely to have seizures when they're given several servings of high-protein puppy food several times a day. Low levels of calcium are rarely a problem because commercial pet foods provide plenty of this mineral. If your dog is nursing, however, your veterinarian may recommend giving her Pet-Tabs or other pet vitamin supplements to keep the calcium levels high.

Record the seizure. If you can keep your hands steady, it's worth videotaping a seizure in progress because veterinarians can sometimes tell by looking at the tape exactly what's causing the problem.

"You'll probably be surprised at how short the seizure really was," Dr. Wallace adds. "A 30-second seizure can seem like an hour."

BREED SPECIFIC

Veterinarians aren't sure why, but German shepherds, Labrador retrievers, Welsh springer spaniels (right), and English springer spaniels have a higher risk of getting epilepsy than other breeds.

Sleeplessness

Dogs have a pretty simple philosophy about life: "When there's nothing else to do, sleep." And they do it very well. The amount of sleep that dogs physically need depends on how active they are. A sheepdog can easily cover 70 miles a day working alongside a farmer, then eat, and sleep until it's time to work again. The average dog leads a sedentary life by comparison, but will still often sleep as much as 18 hours a day, says Joe Betterweck, D.V.M., a veterinarian in private practice in Fresno, California.

Even though routine disturbances—anything from the sound of a mouse scuttering around in a wall cavity to the presence of overnight guests—can keep dogs awake at night, sleeplessness usually occurs when there's something physically wrong, says Dr. Betterweck.

The Usual Suspects

Allergies. Dogs can be allergic to many things, including foods, plants, or airborne dust, molds, and pollen. Some allergies cause digestive problems. More often, dogs with allergies get ferociously itchy, and they may spend hours pacing, whining, or rubbing their faces on the floor. "In the early stages of an allergic reaction, dogs may roll around a lot and be restless and unable to sleep," says Ron Grier, D.V.M., Ph.D., professor of veterinary clinical sciences at Iowa State University in Ames.

Worms and fleas. In the same way that dogs with allergies often get itchy skin, dogs with worms or other parasites may get itchy bottoms. They'll stay awake in order to scratch, usually by scooting their bottoms across the floor, says Dr. Grier. Fleas can be a real problem because many dogs are allergic to the bites and will get so itchy that they can't get to sleep.

Not enough exercise. A well-exercised dog is a tired dog. Conversely,

Dogs who get plenty of regular exercise tend to sleep more soundly than their sedentary counterparts.

127

dogs who lie around the house all day and don't burn off a lot of energy may be too restless to sleep properly at night, says Dr. Grier.

Aches and pains. Many older dogs suffer from arthritis and have trouble finding a comfortable position in which to sleep, says Dr. Grier. In fact, any condition that causes discomfort may be enough to give dogs sleepless nights, he adds.

A full bladder. It's hard for dogs to sleep soundly when they have to keep answering the call of nature. This is often a problem in older dogs, who have less bladder control than when they were younger.

In addition, a key symptom of internal problems such as diabetes and kidney disease is an increased need to urinate, and this in turn leads to disrupted sleep, says Dr. Grier.

Dogs who are suddenly urinating more than usual need to be checked out by a veterinarian. If your dog just happens to have a small bladder, or he's getting to an age where he has to go outside more frequently, the only way to help him sleep is to take him out just before bedtime. At the same time, it may be helpful to limit the amount of water he has available at night to a cup or two.

The Best Care

Get rid of fleas. These little blood-sucking pests are notoriously hard to get rid of. Fleas are prolific breeders, and even when you manage to get rid of adult fleas, there are invariably thousands of babies, in various stages of developing,

CALL FOR HELP

Veterinarians aren't sure what causes it, but a condition called bloat, in which the stomach suddenly fills with air, makes dogs restless and uncomfortable. They'll usually pant a lot, and may have dry heaves as well.

Most common in large, deep-chested dogs such as bullmastiffs (below), Great Danes, and Saint Bernards, bloat causes the stomach to become distended, which can put pressure on major blood vessels around the stomach. You can usually recognize bloat because the abdomen will be uncommonly taut and swollen. Bloat is always an emergency, says Susan Vargas, D.V.M., a veterinarian in private practice in Eugene, Oregon. "Get your dog to the veterinarian as soon as possible," Dr. Vargas advises.

waiting to take their place. Bathing dogs every few weeks, preferably with a flea shampoo, will get rid of a lot of fleas. Dusting or spraying dogs with over-the-counter flea products can be helpful, too.

For a longer-term solution, many experts recommend treating dogs with a product called Frontline, available in pet supply stores and from veterinarians. Applied to the back of a dog's neck where he can't lick it off, Frontline kills fleas and can last as long as a month, says Bernadine Cruz, D.V.M., a veterinarian in private practice in Laguna Hills, California. Even though Frontline kills adult fleas, it isn't effective against fleas at other stages of their life-cycles. For the best flea control, Dr. Cruz recommends combining it with a monthly pill called Program, which circulates in the bloodstream. When adult fleas feed, the medication prevents their eggs from hatching, she explains.

Clean up parasites. Worms and other common parasites thrive in yards and even in carpets and bedding. Regularly vacuuming floors and washing your dog's bedding in hot water once a week will get rid of most parasites. Many more can be eliminated by removing dog stools from the yard each day, says Dr. Cruz. Many parasites live in stools and will reinfest dogs when they come into contact with them, she explains.

Once your dog is infested with worms or other parasites, you'll need to treat him with the proper medication. Over-the-counter products can be very effective, but only if you're sure which parasites your dog has. It's usually easier to take a stool sample to your vet for analysis. Once you know for sure what parasite is involved, you can get the medication that will be most effective—and you and your dog will start sleeping better again, says Dr. Cruz.

Keep the environment clean. Vacuuming and dusting the house, replacing air filters monthly, and using a humidifier will all help rid the air of dust, mold, and other airborne particles that cause allergies, says Dr. Betterweck.

For dogs with arthritis, gently moving their limbs through the full range of motion once a day will help prevent pain that can disrupt their sleep.

Take care of pain. Dogs who hurt will never be able to sleep well, so it's worth trying to make them a little more comfortable.

For dogs with arthritis, gently massage the sore joints and move the limbs through their full range of motion for a few minutes once a day, says Dr. Grier. This will help improve blood flow and keep the muscles and joints limber.

Aspirin helps reduce inflammation as well as pain, making it one of the best arthritis remedies around. Dr. Grier recommends giving dogs a quarter of a 325-milligram tablet for every 10 pounds of weight, once a day.

Applying warmth to the skin with a hot-water bottle wrapped in a towel will provide quick relief from most types of pain. And be sure to put your dog's bed in a warm, draft-free spot, Dr. Grier adds.

Snoring

Nearly all dogs snore occasionally, but the short-nosed breeds such as Pekingese, bulldogs, and pugs tend to be the worst offenders because the shortness of their muzzles may cause chronic breathing problems. Snoring is rarely a sign of serious problems unless dogs are also having trouble breathing when they're awake. But it may suggest that your dog's health—or eating habits—could use some improvements.

The Usual Suspects

Overweight. When dogs are heavier than they should be, they build up an extra layer of fat on the chest. "In some sleeping positions, the extra weight presses on the airways, causing snoring," says Lowell Ackerman, D.V.M., a veterinarian in private practice in Mesa, Arizona.

Obstructions. Dogs often snore when they have a cold, which causes a build-up of mucus in the nose and throat. More seriously, snoring can be caused by polyps or other growths. Some dogs snore when they've been eating plants such as foxtails, bits of which may get caught in their throats, says Lori Teller, D.V.M., a veterinarian in private practice in Houston.

Another cause of obstructions is allergies. Most dogs with allergies have skin reactions, but about 15 percent get the typical human symptoms, such as sneezing and runny eyes and noses. This causes tissues inside the nose to get inflamed and swollen. When their noses get plugged up, dogs breathe through their mouths, and this can make them snore, says Dr. Ackerman.

Aging. In older dogs, tissues near the vocal cords and larynx lose some of their muscle tone, getting thin and loose. The loose tissue vibrates as air passes in and out, says Dr. Ackerman.

Elongated soft palate. The soft palate is the soft flap of tissue that extends from the roof of the mouth into the throat. In short-muzzled breeds such as boxers, bulldogs, and pugs, the soft palate is a bit too long and drops down into the airways. "As these dogs breathe, it sometimes gets sucked into the airways and vibrates, creating the snoring sound," says Ron Grier, D.V.M., Ph.D., professor of veterinary clinical sciences at Iowa State University in Ames.

Dogs who are on the plump side tend to snore more than those who are active and lean.

Veterinarians sometimes recommend surgery when an elongated soft palate is causing medical problems. But most of the time they leave it alone—and the dogs continue snoring.

The Best Care

Put them on a diet. Heavy dogs are much more likely to snore than thin ones. Even if the sound of sawing wood doesn't keep you awake, helping your dog lose weight will be good for his health as well as his sleep. "Cut your dog's food by a quarter and give him more exercise," says Dr. Grier. Most dogs will start losing weight within a few weeks. If your dog doesn't, reduce the food by another quarter. If he still doesn't lose weight, talk to your veterinarian about a more formal weight-loss plan.

Changing foods isn't always helpful, but veterinarians sometimes recommend switching dogs to a food designed for weight loss. These foods are lower in calories than standard dog foods, but they're also high in fiber, which keeps dogs satisfied even when they're eating less.

Relieve the allergies. Even though allergies aren't difficult to treat, it can be a challenge to figure out what dogs are allergic to. Start by removing the most common allergens that can trigger nasal inflammation, such as mold, dust, and pollen. Vacuuming the house and dusting often will remove many of these particles before they have a chance to go airborne.

Another treatment for allergies is to give your dog an over-the-counter human antihistamine, such as Benadryl or Tavist, says Dr. Teller. Veterinarians have found that the medications are effective 25 to 40 percent of the time. The usual dose is one to three milligrams for every pound of weight, but it's a good idea to ask your veterinarian which dose is right for your pet.

 FAST FIX Just like people, some dogs will quit snoring when they sleep in a different position. It doesn't fix the underlying problem but it will give them—and you—some relief. Most dogs like to sleep curled up, but giving them the chance to stretch out—by changing the bed from a round basket to a long mattress, for example—may reduce their breathing difficulties as well as their snoring, says Dr. Grier.

CALL FOR HELP

It's fairly common for dogs to wheeze and gasp when they sleep. Dogs who do it when they're awake, however, could be developing a dangerous condition called laryngeal paralysis, in which the muscles surrounding the opening of the larynx (the upper part of the windpipe) become paralyzed, probably due to inflammation in the nervous or muscular systems. "It doesn't come on suddenly but you can hear a change in your dog's voice when he barks," says Ron Grier, D.V.M., Ph.D., professor of veterinary clinical sciences at Iowa State University in Ames. Dogs with this condition usually pant a lot and tire easily, he adds.

Some dogs will have one or two minor bouts of paralysis and never anything worse. For others, however, the paralysis can be life-threatening, so you'll want to call your vet if you suspect there's a problem.

Squinting

When dogs walk into sunlight after spending time in a darkened room, they will clamp down their eyelids to as narrow a slit as possible. Squinting reduces the intensity of light while the eyes are adjusting to the change.

When squinting lasts more than a second or two, however, you can be pretty sure that something other than too-bright light is irritating the eyes. "There really aren't any harmless things that cause squinting," says John Hamil, D.V.M., a veterinarian in private practice in Laguna Beach, California.

The Usual Suspects

Debris. The eyes are well-protected, but it's very easy for dust or other debris to blow in—and even tiny particles can cause tremendous irritation, says Peggy J. Rucker, D.V.M., a veterinarian in private practice in Lebanon, Virginia. Debris in the eye is even more uncomfortable for dogs than for people. For one thing, dogs don't have fingers to rub away the grit. In addition, they have an anatomical structure called the third eyelid, which hugs the surface of the eye. Designed to protect the eyes from injury, the third eyelid sometimes traps pieces of grit and drags them across the surface of the eye, causing scratches and irritation, Dr. Rucker explains.

Debris in the eye usually washes away in the tears, but dogs may squint for 12 hours or more until the irritation is gone.

Corneal injury. The eyes are covered by a thin, transparent layer of cells called the cornea. Anything that irritates the cornea, from a gritty piece of dust to a minor infection, will cause a lot of pain and squinting.

Vision without Sight

Most people who see Bat for the first time never suspect that the 14-year-old English springer spaniel has been blind since birth. At six weeks of age, he was diagnosed with bilateral congenital glaucoma, a birth defect that causes pressure inside the eyes and destroys the vision cells.

Kay Schwink, D.V.M., a veterinary ophthalmologist in Blacksburg, Virginia, removed the eyes and adopted the blind pup, knowing that he could rely on his senses of smell, hearing, and touch to guide him around his new 100-acre home. Those senses, along with his remarkable ability to memorize the house and land, have guided him through years of an active, happy lifestyle, literally running without boundaries.

Bat maintains regular doggy duties, such as barking out an alarm when cars approach the house and actively defending his territory from unwelcome dogs or rodents. He consistently dodges every fence, barn, and tree as if he can see it. Watching Bat zoom in and out of his doggy door and run free in the green pastures leaves no doubt about his zest for life and his great "vision" of a different kind.

PUPPY DOG TALES

BREED SPECIFIC

Boston terriers, Lhasa apsos, Pekingese, pugs, and shih tzus all have been bred to have protruding eyes. Because the eyes are more-or-less exposed to the elements all the time, these breeds have a high risk of eye injuries.

Dogs with droopy eyes have their own problems. Basset hounds, bloodhounds, and cocker spaniels have a baggy little fold underneath the eyelid. It acts like a collection vat, trapping debris from the tear ducts and sometimes causing irritation.

Conjunctivitis. A delicate membrane called the conjunctiva lines the inner surfaces of the eyelids. This membrane is vulnerable to the same problems as the cornea, including scratches, irritation, and infection. Irritation of the conjunctiva—called conjunctivitis, or pinkeye—results in sore, teary eyes, often with a lot of squinting.

Corneal ulcers. Often caused by irritating substances such as soap or strong shampoo, corneal ulcers are tiny sores that irritate the surface of the eye. They tend to occur in older dogs. Some breeds, such as boxers and Pembroke corgis, have a hereditary risk of getting them, says Dr. Rucker.

Iris atrophy. Another condition that usually occurs in older dogs is iris atrophy, in which the iris—the colored part of the eye that controls the amount of light getting in—begins to shrink. As the iris gets smaller, an uncomfortable amount of light may begin striking nerve fibers in the eyes, and pets will squint to reduce the glare.

Glaucoma. One of the most dangerous causes of squinting, glaucoma causes fluids and pressure within the eye to increase. This often makes dogs squint. Glaucoma can be treated with medications, but it may cause blindness when it isn't detected and treated quickly.

Anterior uveitis. Another condition that causes painful pressure in the eye is anterior uveitis. Often caused by infection, parasites, tumors, injuries, or internal problems such as high blood pressure, it can make the eyes intensely sensitive to light. "Dogs will squint to block out the light," says John Hamil, D.V.M., a veterinarian in private practice in Laguna Beach, California.

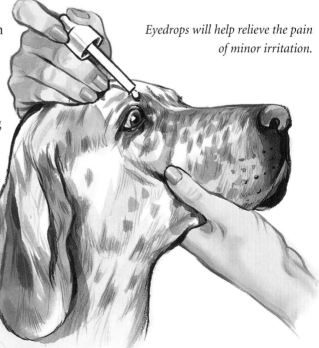

Eyedrops will help relieve the pain of minor irritation.

The Best Care

Flush it out. Regardless of what's causing dogs to squint, it's always worth flushing the eyes with saline solution, says Dr. Rucker. It can't do any harm, and at the very least it will provide a few moments of relief and may wash away whatever is causing the irritation. Hold the eye open with one hand and then flood the surface of the eye with saline with the other. "If your dog is able to hold his eye open a few minutes after the flushing, you've probably been successful in getting rid of whatever was causing the problem," says Dr. Rucker.

Take a closer look. If your dog is still squinting after you've flushed the eye with saline, prop the eyes open, one at a time, and look closely at the brown part to see if there's discoloration or inflammation, says Dr. Rucker. "If there is, it's usually an emergency," she says.

Protect them from glare. Whether they're minor or serious, eye injuries usually make dogs sensitive to bright light. One way to protect the eyes when you're outside is to fit your dog with a visor, available at pet supply stores. A lot of dogs won't put up with them, however, so you may have to keep him indoors during the brightest times of day.

When dogs continue to squint after their eyes have been flushed out, have a close look for any debris or sign of inflammation.

Stiffness

Nearly all dogs get somewhat stiff as they get older, mainly because of gradual wear-and-tear on the joints. And because older dogs gradually become less active, the muscles, ligaments, and tendons tend to lose some of their strength and flexibility.

A little bit of stiffness first thing in the morning isn't likely to be a problem, but you'll want to keep an eye on it because stiffness has a way of getting worse. And you'll definitely want to call your veterinarian when a young dog is having problems because stiffness may be an early sign that the bones and joints aren't developing the way they should.

The Usual Suspects

Arthritis. A painful condition in which inflammation in the joints makes it difficult to move around, arthritis is extremely common, says Lillian Roberts, D.V.M., a veterinarian in private practice in Palm Desert, California. There are a number of different forms of arthritis, but most dogs get either osteoarthritis or rheumatoid arthritis.

Osteoarthritis is caused by a gradual breakdown of bone and cartilage in the joints. Also known as wear-and-tear arthritis, it's usually caused by a lifetime of wear on the joints, most commonly in the hips. Dogs with osteoarthritis tend to have flare-ups of stiffness that last a few hours or days, then gradually get better. In more serious cases, however, the stiffness may never completely go away.

Rheumatoid arthritis is a more serious condition in which the body's immune system, mistaking tissue in the joints as an "invader," sends in destructive cells. Dogs with rheumatoid arthritis may have considerable swelling and inflammation, and without treatment damage to the joints will keep occurring.

Hip dysplasia. The hip joints have a ball-and-socket design, which allows great flexibility and freedom of movement, and are also very strong. In some dogs, however, the hip joints are loose, allowing a lot of play. This condition, called hip dysplasia, causes the various parts of the joint to grind against each other rather than move smoothly, leading to painful inflammation, says Kevin O'Neall, D.V.M., a veterinarian in private practice in Green River, Wyoming. Hip dysplasia is partly hereditary, and is easy to recognize because dogs will have a slight sway when they walk.

The Best Care

Keep them moving. Even dogs who already have arthritis or other joint problems will benefit from regular exercise. It stretches muscles and connective tissues and stimulates the body to release lubricating fluid that helps the joints move more smoothly. And it doesn't take a lot of exercise to deliver benefits. Veterinarians usually recommend two 20-minute walks a day. Doing this regularly not only will help dogs with arthritis feel better but also it may help prevent arthritis from getting started.

Taking a Bead on Pain

Mainstream veterinarians are often reluctant to use holistic care, and Bill Martin, D.V.M., a veterinarian in private practice in Fletcher, North Carolina, was no exception. In fact, he was about to drop out of a short course on acupuncture when his five-year-old miniature dachshund, Blitzen, became paralyzed.

"I called one of the course teachers," Dr. Martin says. "Over the telephone he told me where and how to insert needles in acupuncture points. Within four hours, Blitzen could stand. I immediately decided to continue with the course."

Since then, Dr. Martin has witnessed the benefits of acupuncture time and time again. He remembers Joy, a sweet Doberman pinscher who was in excruciating pain from degenerative disc disease. Dr. Martin decided to use a form of acupuncture in which small gold beads are implanted into acupuncture points. The beads, he explains, constantly stimulate the points, causing the brain to release endorphins to stop the pain. They certainly did the trick for Joy. She walked home that same day—without pain.

PUPPY DOG TALES

You have to be a little careful with young dogs who have hip dysplasia, however. While gentle exercise is helpful, pushing them to go too far or too fast while the joints are still forming can make the hips worse.

Rub the sore spots. Whether stiffness is temporary or a long-term problem, massaging around the hips or wherever else it hurts will increase blood flow and help the body eliminate pain-causing substances from the joints, says Nanette Westhof, D.V.M., a veterinarian in private practice in Mesa, Arizona.

Provide a comfortable bed. Dogs with arthritis usually have their worst moments when they're trying to get up first thing in the morning or when they've been lying down for a while.

You can make the transition a lot more comfortable by giving them the right bed. It should be thick and well-padded and located in a warm, draft-free place. Veterinarians sometimes recommend "egg-carton" mattresses, available at pet supply stores, to help support the joints while dogs sleep.

Keep their weight down. Dogs who are heavier than they should be have a lot more trouble with arthritis simply because their joints are forced to carry more weight than they were designed for. In addition, heavy dogs tend to be lazy dogs, and the lack of exercise invariably makes arthritis worse. Most dogs lose weight fairly easily when they eat about 25 percent less than usual, but you'll want to ask your veterinarian to design a customized weight-loss plan.

FAST FIX For occasional stiffness, aspirin can make a big difference, says Dr. Westhof. It reduces pain, of course, but it also blocks chemicals in the body that cause inflammation. The usual dose is one-quarter of a 325-milligram tablet for every 10 pounds of weight, given once or twice a day.

Aspirin may cause stomach upsets in some dogs, so talk to your veterinarian before giving it at home, says Dr. Westhof. It's best to give buffered or coated aspirin. Don't substitute other types of anti-inflammatory medications, some of which may be harmful for dogs.

Straining to Urinate

With their natural attraction to fire hydrants, trees, and any patch of grass, dogs use their bathroom breaks as a sort of mini-vacation. They urinate happily and often. But sometimes what should come naturally becomes painful and unnaturally slow and difficult. Straining to urinate means that something is interfering with the normal flow of urine, and it's potentially quite serious.

The Usual Suspects

Urinary tract infections. Dogs with urinary tract infections will get sudden and frequent urges to urinate. They'll usually strain even when their bladders are almost empty. Caused by bacteria in the bladder or urethra (the tube through which urine flows), urinary

Older female dogs are particularly prone to urinary tract infections. Encouraging them to drink more water will help flush out the bacteria that cause infections.

tract infections make urinating very painful. Any dog can get an infection, but they're more common in females because their urethras are shorter, making it easier for bacteria to get upstream. Dogs with infections usually have dark, cloudy-looking urine, possibly tinged with green or red. It will also have a strong smell, says Dan Carey, D.V.M., a veterinarian with the Iams pet food company in Dayton, Ohio.

Prostate problems. The prostate gland, which encircles the urethra at the entrance to the bladder, is responsible for producing semen. It's common for the prostate gland to get larger as dogs get older. As it swells, it may put pressure on the urethra, making urination difficult. Dogs with swollen or infected prostate glands will sometimes have blood in the urine as well. Prostate infections are usually treated with antibiotics, while veterinarians recommend neutering for dogs with prostate enlargement.

Bladder stones. The urine is full of minerals, which usually pass in the liquid out of the body. But sometimes minerals in the bladder clump together, forming bladder stones. These stones, also called uroliths, usually occur when dogs are four to six years old.

The Best Care

Flush out the system. Dogs who drink a lot of water are less likely to get bladder stones because the minerals in the bladder will be less concentrated. At a minimum, dogs need to drink one ounce of water for every pound of

Giving dogs plenty of chances to get outside for bathroom breaks will reduce their risk of developing bladder stones.

of sodium, which can make their conditions worse, adds Dr. Carey.

Let them out often. The bladder is a strong muscle and is very elastic, and most dogs can hold on for up to 12 hours, if necessary. But the longer dogs go in between bathroom breaks, the higher the risk of developing bladder stones, says Dr. Carey. At a minimum, dogs should go outside three or four times a day. If you're away from home a lot, the best solution may be to fit a doggy door, which will allow them to heed Nature's call at their convenience. Training your dog to urinate on newspapers in a designated part of the house can also solve the problem if he has to be left alone for long periods.

Acidify the urine. Some of the bacteria that cause urinary tract infections can't thrive in an acidic environment, which is why veterinarians sometimes recommend switching dogs to premium pet foods. These foods have high levels of

weight each day. Dogs with bladder stones need to drink even more to flush out the urinary tract, says Dr. Carey. Dogs don't always drink as much as they should, however. You can encourage them to drink more by adding a pinch of salt to their food, he advises. They like the taste, and the salt will make them thirstier.

Switch to bottled water. Dogs with bladder stones will sometimes improve when they're switched to low-mineral, or soft, bottled water, says Dr. Carey. Tap water and some bottled spring waters are high in calcium, which can lead to the formation of stones in the bladder.

Dogs who have heart problems or who suffer from fluid retention shouldn't be given soft water because it contains high levels

BREED SPECIFIC

Dogs who are most vulnerable to bladder stones include schnauzers, miniature poodles, dachshunds, Dalmatians, cocker spaniels, and pugs. Terriers, basset hounds, corgis (left), and bulldogs have a high risk, too.

CALL FOR HELP

Dogs who are repeatedly straining—and failing—to urinate for more than 12 hours need to see a veterinarian right away because the flow of urine is probably completely blocked, says Dan Carey, D.V.M., a veterinarian with the Iams pet food company in Dayton, Ohio.

Most likely, a bladder stone has migrated from the bladder into the urethra and is blocking the flow, so that urine backs up in the bladder. Your veterinarian can usually relieve the pressure in a few minutes by inserting a catheter into the bladder, says Dr. Carey, and dogs will leave the office in much better spirits. Once the immediate pain is relieved, the vet will need to remove the stone and analyze it. There are about a dozen different types of bladder stones, depending on the accumulation of minerals that's causing the problem, and each needs a different course of treatment. Some can be dissolved with prescription diets, while others must be removed surgically.

take 500 milligrams a day, and larger dogs can take 750 to 1,000 milligrams a day. Capsules or tablets are the best way of giving dogs vitamin C—they don't like the taste of the crystalline form. Some dogs get diarrhea after taking vitamin C, Dr. Scholey adds. It may be necessary to reduce the dose until you find an amount that won't upset your dog's system.

Give cranberry concentrate. This traditional human treatment for urinary tract infections appears to work for dogs as well, provided it's taken in the early stages of the infection, says Dr. Scholey. She recommends giving dogs with urinary tract infections cranberry extract in capsule form, which can inhibit the growth of bacteria in the bladder and help dogs recover more quickly. Small dogs can take one capsule a day, medium-size dogs one capsule twice a day, and large dogs can have one capsule three times a day. Capsules are more effective than fresh juice because the extract they contain is more concentrated, says Dr. Scholey.

animal protein, which makes the urine a little more acidic, Dr. Carey explains.

Give them vitamin C. Another way to acidify the urine is to give dogs vitamin C, also called ascorbic acid, says Anna Scholey, D.V.M., a veterinarian in private practice in Dallas. She recommends giving 250 milligrams of vitamin C a day to dogs weighing under 20 pounds. Dogs up to 50 pounds can

If you can't let your dog out frequently, one solution is to teach him to urinate on newspapers.

Swallowing Difficulties

Dogs are constantly picking things up in their mouths, giving an exploratory chew or two, and delivering judgment: "Tasty" or "No good." When the verdict is favorable, they'll usually try to swallow whatever it is they're sampling—a piece of paper, a small stone, or a bit of bone. This is normal dog behavior, which means that struggling to swallow is a symptom you'll probably see quite a bit. It's so common, in fact, that people tend to take no notice of it—which is a mistake, because difficulty swallowing is also a symptom of more serious problems.

The Usual Suspects

Obstructions. Anything that gets stuck in the throat or esophagus—the tube that leads from the throat to the stomach—will cause dogs to swallow repeatedly as they try to make it go down. "The variety of things that vets have found stuck in the mouth, throat, or esophagus is endless," says Taylor Wallace, D.V.M., a veterinarian in private practice in Seattle. "Dogs will try to eat anything: corn cobs, balls, nails, rocks, string, bones, coins, and rawhide chews," she says.

Dogs may also have trouble swallowing their food, especially when they eat voraciously and ingest more at a time than they can comfortably handle. This has become more of a problem in recent years as people have begun feeding their dogs whole, unprocessed meats, such as chicken legs. Dogs who don't take their time chewing may find themselves struggling just to swallow the last bite.

Growths or tumors. It doesn't happen very often, but dogs sometimes develop growths inside the esophagus, says Dr. Wallace. The growths can be benign or they can be cancerous. Either way, they're uncomfortable, causing dogs to repeatedly swallow.

Infections. "Infections in the nose, mouth, throat, or tonsils can make it painful and difficult for dogs to swallow," says Agnes Rupley, D.V.M., a veterinarian in private practice in College Station, Texas. The infections don't have to be serious to cause problems, she adds. Even a minor sinus infection can result in postnasal drip, forcing a dog to keep swallowing.

Pebbles

Fishing sinkers

Coins

String

Some dogs will eat almost anything, including things that are difficult or dangerous to swallow.

BREED SPECIFIC

Labrador retrievers (left), poodles, and terriers have been bred for generations to use their mouths—for retrieving downed birds, for example. As a result, they like to hold things in their mouths, and sometimes they accidentally swallow them, too.

Damaged esophagus. Dogs don't get heartburn the way people do, but they do sometimes eat caustic substances or lap up toilet water that contains chemical cleaners. Harsh chemicals can burn the esophagus, and dogs will repeatedly swallow to try to relieve the burn, says Rance Sellon, D.V.M., a veterinarian specializing in internal medicine at Washington State University in Pullman.

Lumps and sores. "A lump or sore in the mouth may interfere with the muscle and nerve function needed for normal swallowing," says Dr. Sellon. Caused by problems ranging from minor cuts to immune system illnesses, lumps or sores in the mouth can make swallowing difficult, he explains.

Nausea. Since dogs love scavenging for extra (and preferably smelly) meals, they get nauseated almost as often as they eat what they shouldn't. Dogs who look as though they're having trouble swallowing may be sick to their stomachs, says Dr. Wallace. "The nausea makes dogs salivate and swallow a lot," she says.

The Best Care

Get a good look. If your dog has been swallowing normally, but suddenly seems to be having a problem, there's a good chance something is stuck in the mouth or throat. Veterinarians recommend holding your dog's mouth open with one hand and pointing a flashlight inside with the other. Look around the teeth, lips, and tongue, and along the roof of the mouth to see if something's there. And take a long look at the

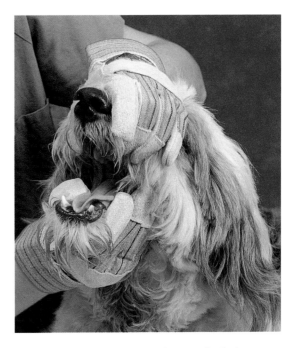

Things can get stuck in several parts of a dog's mouth—around his teeth, across the roof of his mouth, or at the back of the throat. When taking a look, wear sturdy gloves in case he bites down.

CALL FOR HELP

Dogs often get things stuck in their throats. Most of the time a few gags and hacks will pop the objects right out. But you can't assume that obstructions will automatically free themselves, says Jerry Woodfield, D.V.M., a veterinary cardiologist in private practice in Seattle. Since dogs who are having trouble swallowing may also be having trouble breathing, you need to watch carefully to see what's happening. "Be sure his gums are pink," says Dr. Woodfield. Dogs with pink gums have plenty of oxygen in their blood. Gums that turn dark, usually dark blue or purple, mean that the body is low on oxygen and you have an emergency on your hands.

The tissues that line the mouth and throat are very delicate, which is why veterinarians advise being extremely careful about removing anything but the simplest objects. A stick caught between the teeth is no big deal, but something stuck in the throat or wedged tightly in the mouth needs to be dealt with by a professional, says Agnes Rupley, D.V.M., a veterinarian in private practice in College Station, Texas. "Anything like string, dental floss, or fishing line can be a real problem," she adds. "They act like tiny knives, making lots of minute cuts if you try to pull them out."

on the roof of the mouth. Objects farther in, or objects that won't come out easily, may need to be professionally removed.

"If you can't see all of it, don't try to pull it out yourself," says Dr. Sellon.

Dogs don't like having their mouths held open and will try mightily to close them—which means you could get bitten if you aren't careful. With large dogs especially, or those with sharp teeth, wear heavy gloves while giving them the once-over, advises Dr. Sellon. If your dog fights too hard, it's probably easier—and safer—just to take him to the vet, he adds.

Give him soft food. Since even mild sores or infections can make it hard for dogs to swallow for a few days, they may not eat enough to get all the nutrients they need in order to heal. "For dogs that eat dry food, soften it with water," suggests Dr. Wallace. "If it's canned food he likes, add water to make a dog-food soup."

Give them ice to eat. Most dogs love to crunch on ice, and the cool chips will help numb and soothe a sore throat, says Dr. Wallace. You can give them ice by itself, or mix the ice in a bit of water to make a sore-throat slush, she says.

Neutralize the acids. Since you can't see the esophagus without special instruments, there's no way to tell whether or not it's been damaged. If your vet suspects that a damaged esophagus is causing the swallowing difficulties, he may recommend giving your dog Pepcid AC, an over-the-counter product that decreases stomach acid and helps reduce nausea and vomiting, says Dr. Sellon.

However, be sure to check with your vet before you use an antacid. "Not all over-the-counter antacids are the same," he warns.

back of the throat, which is where objects often get lodged. Many objects are easy to remove, especially if they're stuck between the teeth or

Swollen Joints

Every joint in your dog's body, from the elbows to the hips, has a number of moving parts. When something goes wrong with one or more of those parts, the body sends in blood and other fluids to control the damage. This is what causes joints to swell.

Swelling is always painful and occasionally serious. "If a dog is simply limping and has a little bit of stiffness and maybe even a little bit of swelling, I don't think it's unreasonable to wait 24 to 48 hours for it to get better with rest," says John Hamil, D.V.M., a veterinarian in private practice in Laguna Beach, California. "But if it fails to get better, then it definitely ought to be seen by a veterinarian."

The Usual Suspects

Injuries. In puppies and older dogs especially, hard exercise can strain the tissues surrounding joints, causing painful swelling, says Dr. Hamil.

BREED SPECIFIC

Large- and giant-breed puppies, such as Irish wolfhounds (right), often have voracious appetites. This can be a problem because if they gain too much weight too quickly, they can damage cartilage in the shoulder or other joints, a condition called osteochondritis dissecans.

Infections. Sometimes an infection is local—that is, it is limited to one particular joint. This usually occurs when there has been an injury because of a fight with another dog, for example, or a deep cut or puncture has allowed bacteria to get into the joint.

Infections can also spread throughout the body, causing swelling in a number of different joints. For instance, pets who have Lyme disease, a bacterial infection that is transmitted by ticks, often have trouble walking because many of their joints may be swollen and painful at the same time.

Arthritis. Usually a problem in older dogs, arthritis often causes joints to swell. One kind of arthritis, called osteoarthritis or degenerative

These young Labradors will wrestle and tumble all day—and sometimes they'll pay for their exuberance with swollen joints.

143

joint disease, is simply the result of years of normal wear and tear.

A more serious form of arthritis, called rheumatoid arthritis, occurs when the immune system periodically attacks tissue inside the joints, causing painful swelling.

Cancer. This is probably the most serious cause of joint swelling. Veterinarians have made tremendous progress in treating cancer, but treatments will always be most effective when the cancer is detected early. It's always worth calling your veterinarian when there's swelling that doesn't go away within a few days, even if it doesn't seem to be causing discomfort.

Hip dysplasia. A very common problem in large dogs, hip dysplasia is an inherited condition in which the hip bones don't fit together as tightly as they should. Hip dysplasia usually begins in the first six months of a dog's life, although the pain and stiffness generally don't appear until much later.

Dogs with hip dysplasia don't always have visible swelling. But the condition often leads to arthritis, which can cause swelling that may be easy to see. One way to spot hip dysplasia is to watch how dogs move. They may start to have trouble getting up and will have a distinctive sway when they walk.

The Best Care

Check for infection. Since any infection needs to be treated by a veterinarian, you need to figure out if that's what's causing the swelling. Try feeling the joint. If it's warmer than the surrounding area and there's a bit of redness beneath the fur, it is probably infected.

Reduce the discomfort. Joint swelling is potentially risky, so it's not something you want to ignore. One way to help reduce the swelling a little and make your dog more comfortable is to put a cold pack, or ice wrapped in a washcloth, on the swollen area several times a day for about 10 minutes each time. This reduces the flow of blood to the joint, which can bring the swelling down. When swelling is due to arthritis, on the other hand, warm wraps will keep relieve the pain. However, they won't have much effect on the swelling.

Keep the joints moving. Swollen joints are usually painful, so you don't want to push your dog into more activity than he's comfortable with. But it's still a good idea to get him moving at least a little bit because exercise increases

Joints that are swelling enough to cause discomfort are usually easy to feel—and this Maltese is enjoying the attention.

CALL FOR HELP

Even though joint swelling is common and often goes away on its own, there's always the risk that it's caused by a serious infection deep within the joint. It's impossible to tell at home when this is happening, which is why veterinarians recommend getting help within a day or two if it doesn't go away.

Veterinarians usually treat infections by giving antibiotics. In some cases, though, they may have to drain pus and other fluids from the joint with a syringe. Dogs taking antibiotics will usually feel better and move with less discomfort within a day, although it usually takes about two weeks to knock out the underlying infection.

Keep them warm. Dogs with swollen joints get even stiffer and more sore when they sleep on hard surfaces or beds that aren't supportive enough, so you'll want to fix them up with a warm, well-padded place to lie down. For dogs who spend a lot of time outdoors, some veterinarians recommend shopping for a heated pet bed, which will keep them comfortable even on the chilliest days.

FAST FIX The quickest way to reduce swelling as well as pain is to give dogs a little aspirin. The usual dose is 10 milligrams of coated or buffered aspirin for every pound of your dog's weight, given once or twice a day. Buffered aspirin is less likely to upset the stomach. Some dogs, though, can't tolerate aspirin at all, so be sure to check with your vet before giving it at home.

blood flow, which helps remove fluids from swollen areas while allowing fresh blood and nutrients to get in.

Make life convenient. To keep dogs comfortable until the swelling goes down, veterinarians recommend putting their food and water bowls nearby, so they don't have to walk as far. And since dogs with swollen joints often have trouble getting about on slippery floors or steep steps, it is a good idea to do a little temporary remodeling, such as putting down throw rugs on wood or tile floors to make it easier for them to get traction. Dogs need to go outside to do their business no matter how stiff and sore they might feel, so if there are steps leading down to the backyard, you may want to put down a simple carpeted ramp as well.

Keeping dogs warm is one way to reduce uncomfortable stiffness. These whippets have cosy quilted jackets to keep their joints limber.

Swollen Stomach

Dogs love to eat, and sometimes they pay for their hearty appetites by getting noticeably rotund. Unlike many humans, however, overweight pets don't just get a big stomach—they get round all over.

A dog whose stomach is taut and swollen is almost always sick. If there's no chance that pregnancy is the reason, you'll need to investigate and treat other possible causes.

The Usual Suspects

Parasites. Puppies who get a big belly almost always have worms, says Kristin Varner, D.V.M., a veterinarian in private practice in

It's normal for puppies to be plump, but if they're really potbellied, they probably have worms.

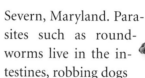

BREED SPECIFIC

Bloat usually occurs in large dogs with deep chests, such as Great Danes, Saint Bernards, golden and Labrador retrievers, Weimaraners (right), and Irish setters.

Severn, Maryland. Parasites such as roundworms live in the intestines, robbing dogs of essential protein. When protein levels fall, pets may begin secreting fluids into the abdomen, causing a potbelly.

Bloat. When the stomach swells up in the space of an hour or two, it's usually because of bloat, a life-threatening condition in which the stomach fills with gas that can't escape, says Thomas Schmidt, D.V.M., a veterinarian in private practice in Fort Washington, Maryland.

Veterinarians aren't sure what causes bloat, also called gastric dilatation-volvulus. It usually occurs after large meals and is most common in large, deep-chested dogs. It's dangerous because accumulations of gas can cause the stomach to twist and close off, trapping the gas and putting pressure on major blood vessels.

Abdominal fluid. It's normal for dogs to have small amounts of fluid in the abdomen, just enough to keep the organs moist. But pets with internal problems such as cancer or liver or heart disease will often retain fluids, causing their bellies to swell to several times their normal size, a condition called ascites, says Dan Carey, D.V.M., a veterinarian with the Iams pet food company in Dayton, Ohio.

Hormonal problems. In dogs with a condition called Cushing's disease, the adrenal glands churn out too much hormone, which can cause the abdomen to swell. Cushing's disease weakens the abdominal muscles, so the stomach may droop toward the ground as well. Cushing's disease is usually treated by giving dogs medications that cause the adrenal gland to produce less hormone.

Pregnancy. One of the most obvious causes of a potbelly—but one which many owners forget to consider—is pregnancy. From the time a pet starts to show to the time she delivers, her belly may double or even triple in size. So if you have an unspayed female, and if there's even a chance she could have had an unauthorized visitor, you may want to ask your vet if she might be expecting.

The Best Care

Check for parasites. Worms are usually easy to spot by looking at the stools and the fur around the anal area. Roundworms resemble long strands of spaghetti and are easy to see. Tapeworms look a bit like grains of rice—these are broken-off segments of the worms.

Over-the-counter deworming products containing pyrantel pamoate are effective and safe as long as you follow the directions exactly.

The problem with treating worms yourself, cautions Dr. Varner, is that pets with one kind of parasite often have other kinds as well. The medications you buy at the pet supply store won't kill all of them. Your best bet is to call your vet, she advises.

Get rid of bloat. Bloat is always an emergency and you need to get help as quickly as possible, says Susan Vargas, D.V.M., a veterinarian in private practice in Eugene, Oregon. Your

POOCH PUZZLER

Can puppies from the same litter have different fathers?

When pregnancies have been planned and supervised, it's easy to know who the father of the puppies is. In some unplanned matings, however, it's a different story.

Female dogs in heat are irresistibly attractive to males. If a female in heat isn't kept inside or securely enclosed, a pack of males will quickly gather and fight for the privilege of mating. These fights will identify the dominant dog, and he's the one that the female is most likely to choose.

After the mating, the male will usually hang around the female to guard her—and his biological investment—from rivals. But if the mated pair becomes separated, or the male can't defend his mate, she may hook up with another suitor. Since she has no guarantee that the first male was fertile, choosing a backup mate will increase her chances of becoming pregnant. When both males are fertile, however, she'll end up with pups that have two different fathers.

veterinarian will usually get rid of the accumulated gas by passing a tube down the throat into the stomach.

You can't treat bloat at home, but there are ways to help ensure that it never comes back. Dr. Carey recommends switching dogs to a "high performance" food, one that has about 20 percent fat. This is a higher percentage of fat than is contained in regular foods, which means dogs will eat less—and eating less can help prevent bloat, he says.

Dr. Carey also recommends feeding dogs several small meals a day rather than one big meal. "Breaking the food down into two or three servings will reduce the amount of food and water the stomach needs to handle at one time," he explains. Elevating your dog's food dishes will also help prevent bloat by reducing the amount of air he gulps down while he's eating or drinking.

Veterinarians aren't sure why, but dogs have a higher risk for developing bloat when they eat shortly before or after exercising. Dr. Carey recommends not letting dogs eat or drink a lot of water for at least an hour before having vigorous exercise. After meals, they should wait at least two hours before exercising.

Raising a dog's food and water dishes will help prevent large amounts of air from being swallowed, which can increase the risk of bloat.

CALL FOR HELP

Bloat is a life-threatening condition that develops very quickly. It's not uncommon for dogs to go from being perfectly normal to desperately ill in just a few hours—or even less. That's why people with big, deep-chested dogs—dogs who have the highest risk of bloat—need to be able to recognize the signs that it's coming on, says Susan Vargas, D.V.M., a veterinarian in private practice in Eugene, Oregon.

Symptoms of bloat include:

- The belly is taut and swollen.
- Your dog is restless, lethargic, or visibly uncomfortable.
- He's panting heavily.
- One side of the body seems rigid.

"Once you've seen bloat, you'll always know what it is," says Dr. Vargas. And because bloat is such a dangerous condition, you need to get your dog to a veterinarian immediately, she says.

Urinating Less Often

There is a great deal of variability in the frequency with which dogs urinate. Dogs with small bladders will need to urinate more often than those with larger capacities, and older dogs usually urinate more than younger ones. But dogs are very predictable in their habits, especially when it comes to asking to be let outside. A dog who's suddenly urinating less than usual may have a potentially serious problem, and you'll want to call your veterinarian right away.

The Usual Suspects

Fever. Dogs with viral infections can develop high fevers just as people do. They'll often urinate less while they're sick because the fever is burning up more fluids internally, says L. R. Danny Daniel, D.V.M., a veterinarian in private practice in Covington, Louisiana.

Dehydration. In hot weather especially, dogs don't always get enough to drink—if only because they have a habit of tipping over their water bowls after the people in the family have gone to work. Going without water for a few hours isn't likely to hurt them, but it doesn't take long for them to get dehydrated—and the body responds by conserving fluids. "You may not be filling the water bowl often enough," says Dr. Daniel.

Urinary tract infections. Dogs with infections in the bladder or urethra usually urinate more rather than less. In some cases, however, infections weaken the bladder, making it hard

for this large muscle to push urine out. A similar problem occurs if spinal nerves get damaged or compressed—by an injured spinal disc, for example. Pressure on the nerves can block the impulses that tell the body when it's time to urinate.

Kidney disease. The kidneys are responsible for filtering many of the body wastes and eliminating them in the urine. Dogs will urinate

Dogs don't always drink as much as they should to keep the urinary tract healthy. Some people get very creative about encouraging their dogs to drink. These Australian shepherds always enjoy drinking cool water from a hose.

149

less when the kidneys aren't working as efficiently as they should. "Pets with kidney disease can get quite sick as fluids and wastes build up," explains Dr. Daniel.

The Best Solutions

Check for fever. Most viral infections aren't very serious, but it's important to know whether it's just a fever that's causing your dog to urinate less frequently or whether something else is going on. You can check your dog's temperature with a rectal thermometer lubricated with a little petroleum or K-Y Jelly.

The normal temperature for dogs is between 99.5°F and 102.5°F. When the temperature rises above 103°F, they have a fever, and you'll want to call your vet, says Beverly J. Scott, D.V.M., a veterinarian in private practice in Gilbert, Arizona.

Provide extra fluids. You can't force dogs to drink more water, but keeping the bowl filled with fresh, cool water, especially in the warm months or when they're more active than usual, will entice them to drink their fill.

Drinking more water does more than reverse dehydration, Dr. Daniel adds. It also helps flush bacteria from the bladder and urinary tract, which can help prevent urinary tract infections as well as reduce irritation in dogs who already are infected.

FAST FIX The body has a thirst mechanism that's responsible for telling dogs when to drink more. This mechanism isn't always as effective as it should be, however, which is why veterinarians sometimes recommend tickling a dog's thirst in another

CALL FOR HELP

Since one of the main symptoms of kidney disease is urinating less often, you don't want to wait for more than a day or two before calling your veterinarian. Before you take your dog in, however, your vet may ask you to collect a urine sample at home. Dogs don't urinate on command, and the checkup will be less productive without the sample. Vets can tell a lot just by looking at the urine, says L. R. Danny Daniel, D.V.M., a veterinarian in private practice in Covington, Louisiana.

Urine may become dark and concentrated when dogs aren't drinking enough water because there isn't a lot of fluid in the urine to dilute the wastes.

The urine often gets very light or even clear in dogs with kidney problems. Urine that's consistently very clear may be a sign that wastes are staying in the body instead of being concentrated in the urine.

Kidney problems always need medical attention, says Dr. Daniel. Some dogs will be given dialysis to remove toxins from the body. In addition, your vet will probably recommend a low-protein diet. Part of the kidneys' job is filtering protein by-products. Giving your pet foods that are low in protein will put less strain on the kidneys, he explains.

way—by putting extra flavor in the water. If your dog starts drinking more and his urinary habits return to normal, you can be pretty confident that he just needed to drink a little more.

Urinating Too Frequently

Most dogs urinate three or four times a day, not counting the endless pit stops they make at telephone poles or on patches of grass in order to mark their territory or pass along greetings to other dogs. As with most bodily functions, however, there really isn't such a thing as "normal" urination. Some dogs are comfortable going two or three times a day. For others, especially hard-working dogs who drink a lot of water, seven, eight, or nine times a day isn't unusual, says Christine Wilford, D.V.M., a veterinarian in private practice in Edmonds, Washington.

It isn't the frequency of urination that gets a veterinarian's attention as much as changes in frequency. Dogs who start urinating much more often than usual invariably have a physical problem. Either something is blocking or irritating the urinary tract, or there's an internal problem that's causing the body to eliminate more fluids.

The Usual Suspects

Infection or irritation. Infections can occur anywhere in the urinary tract, from the urethra (the tube through which urine leaves the body) all the way up to the bladder or even the kidneys. Infections don't always cause the body to produce more urine, but they do irritate the urinary tract, increasing the urge to urinate, says Bonnie Wilcox, D.V.M., a veterinarian in private practice in Preemption, Illinois.

Dogs with infections or other types of irritation will often be desperate to go outside, even though they may release only a few drops when they get there. The urine may have a strong, fishy smell as well.

Obstructions. Dogs commonly get bladder stones, hard little crystals that form when minerals in the urine clump together. The stones can get quite large and may cause irritation that leads to frequent urination, pain, or bleeding, says Dr. Wilford. Should a stone migrate out of the bladder into the urethra, it may block the flow of urine.

Although male dogs don't get stones more often than females, they do have a greater chance of urethral obstructions because their urethras are longer and thinner than those in females. "They will seem to be urinating frequently, but

CALL FOR HELP

Veterinarians worry when unspayed female dogs suddenly start urinating a lot because they could have pyometra, a dangerous infection of the uterus that requires emergency care, says Christine Wilford, D.V.M., a veterinarian in private practice in Edmonds, Washington. Pyometra usually occurs within three months of a heat cycle, and surgery to remove the uterus is usually required. Other internal problems that may cause frequent urination include diabetes, kidney or liver disease, and some hormone imbalances, Dr. Wilford adds.

if you watch, you'll see that no urine will come out, or only teensy dribbles," says Dr. Wilford. And they'll appear agitated and in pain.

Age. Dogs often urinate more as they get older because they can't hold on for as long as they could when they were younger. They also have a higher risk of incontinence, which usually occurs when the urinary sphincter, the muscle that controls when urine leaves the bladder, gets weaker over time. Spayed females are especially prone to incontinence because they produce very little estrogen, a hormone that helps keep the muscles in the urinary tract strong. Older spayed females sometimes need estrogen supplements, says Dr. Wilcox.

The Best Care

Drink away infections. It seems paradoxical that dogs who are urinating a lot will improve after drinking more water, but the extra fluids can help flush infection-causing bacteria from the bladder, says Dr. Wilford. Water also reduces the concentration of minerals and other irritating substances in the urine, and this in turn can reduce the need to urinate so often.

Since it's a challenge to get dogs to drink additional water, veterinarians recommend making their usual water more appetizing—by adding beef or chicken broth, for example, or even a tablespoon of clam juice from a can, says Dr. Wilford. The slight saltiness will encourage them to drink even more, she explains. You can also get more liquid into their bodies by adding about a quarter-cup of water or other fluids to their food.

Letting a bladder infection go untreated can lead to kidney infections or bladder stones, says

Encouraging dogs to drink more fluids can help dilute the concentration of irritating substances in their urine, and also help to flush away bacteria.

Dr. Wilford. Dogs who are still urinating frequently after two days should get a checkup. Urinary infections respond readily to antibiotics, which will usually stop the symptoms within a few days and entirely eliminate the infection within a week or two.

It's important to always finish the whole course of antibiotics and to return for a checkup to ensure that the urine is completely clear of infection, Dr. Wilford adds.

Dissolve the stones. Large urinary stones usually need to be removed surgically, but smaller stones will sometimes dissolve—or fail to form entirely—when you give dogs more water and change what goes in their food bowls. There are two distinct types of stones.

• Struvite stones, which typically form after dogs have had infections, can sometimes be

Any kind of exercise will help strengthen the muscles that control urination, but swimming is particularly good for older dogs because it's easy on the joints.

broken down in the bladder by switching dogs to a low-protein, low-ash, and high-salt dog food. This type of diet, available by prescription from veterinarians, isn't recommended for preventing stones, however, says Dr. Wilford.

• Uric acid stones may form when a protein by-product (uric acid) isn't completely broken down in the liver. This condition is most common in Dalmatians. Dogs who are prone to these stones are often given a prescription diet that helps prevent them. For some dogs, stones can be controlled with the diet alone, but other dogs may also need medication.

Keep them active. Exercise strengthens every muscle in the body, including the muscles that control urination. Older dogs who are hav-ing trouble controlling their bladders may im-prove when they're taken for two 30-minute walks a day, says Dr. Wilcox. Swimming is a par-ticularly good form of exercise for older dogs because even though it's strenuous, the water helps support aging joints.

TAKING A URINE SAMPLE

When treating dogs with urinary problems, veterinarians usually begin by analyzing a urine sample. Dogs aren't at their most cooperative once they're at the vet's, so it's worth trying to collect a urine sample before you leave home, says Bonnie Wilcox, D.V.M., a veterinarian in private practice in Preemption, Illinois. It's best to take the sample first thing in the morning, when the urine is at its most concentrated, she adds. Here's a simple, mess-free way to collect a specimen from your dog.

• Tape a paper cup to the end of a piece of wire from a clothes hanger.

• Put your dog on a leash and walk her to her usual "spot." As soon as the knees bend or the leg lifts, slip the paper cup into position.

• Transfer the urine to a clean, airtight container and take it to your veterinarian within three to four hours.

Vomiting

When it comes to eating, dogs love to experiment. They'll eat trash, rotten potatoes, entire bags of candy, or anything else that they're lucky enough to discover. Nature made allowance for their adventurous appetites by giving them the ability to empty their stomachs on a moment's notice. "Dogs can vomit almost by just thinking about it," says Dan Carey, D.V.M., a veterinarian with the Iams pet food company in Dayton, Ohio.

The Usual Suspects

Dietary indiscretions. The main reason dogs vomit is that they've eaten something that their stomachs aren't equipped to handle, such as mouthfuls of grass or spoiled food from the trash can. Even perfectly wholesome food can make them sick when they eat too much of it—which is why most people eventually decide to keep the dog food bag out of sight behind cupboard doors.

Spoiled foods. Commercial pet foods have impressive storage abilities, but once they've been moistened with water, they can go bad in as little as three hours. Canned food may "turn" even

A few blackberries are unlikely to harm this sable Border collie, but other dogs are often led astray by their adventurous appetites, eating things that disagree with them.

faster. Dogs aren't put off by strong odors, so spoiled foods are perfectly acceptable to their tastebuds, if not their stomachs.

Swallowed objects. Dogs don't usually mean to swallow marbles, plastic toys, bottle caps, or any of the other objects that they sniff, nose around, and put in their mouths. But many things that go in the mouth end up going down the hatch—and the stomach may respond by sending them right back up.

Worms. Intestinal parasites such as roundworms, tapeworms, and whipworms live in the digestive tract, and sometimes they cause so much irritation that dogs get sick and start vomiting. Worms are very common in puppies, who often get infected before they're born. You can buy worming medications in pet supply stores and from veterinarians.

Ulcers. Dogs don't have a lot of stress in their lives, but they still can get ulcers—usually

UP IT COMES

Dogs will sample almost anything they can find, even poisons. If you know that a dog has swallowed a noncorrosive poison such as antifreeze or a human medication, you'll want to help him throw it up. With a bulb syringe or a turkey baster, slowly drip 3 percent hydrogen peroxide solution (available from drugstores) into the side of the mouth. Use one tablespoon for every 20 pounds of body weight. Then get veterinary help right away.

because they ate something that damaged the lining of the stomach, such as pennies or small batteries. Dogs with ulcers will often throw up material that looks like coffee grounds, which is a sign that they're throwing up digested blood.

Morning sickness. Occasionally, dogs bring up a little yellow liquid when they wake up in the morning. It looks ugly, but it isn't serious. Vets call this bilious vomiting, and it's caused by going all night without food. Basically, it just means that their stomachs are upset.

The Best Care

Give the stomach a rest. Just as it's important to rest a muscle that's been overworked, the stomach also needs a rest when it's been turning upside down. Veterinarians recommend not letting dogs eat for at least 12 hours after they've been sick. Otherwise, their still-queasy stomachs will probably just toss it up again. If the vomiting has stopped after 12 hours or so, it's fine to give them a little bit of food again—about an

eighth of their usual amount, says Dr. Carey. A few hours later, give them a little more. The idea is to let their stomachs slowly get back to normal while maintaining a healthful diet. Most dogs will be back at their normal amounts within two to three days, he says.

Limit the water they drink. Dogs who have been sick need to drink to replace the fluids that vomiting has removed. But you don't want them to drink too much water because it will irritate the stomach, says Lila Miller, D.V.M., senior director of animal sciences and veterinary adviser to the American Society for the Prevention of Cruelty to Animals in New York City. She recommends letting them take a few laps from the bowl, and then putting the bowl out of reach for a while. An hour later, let them drink a little more, she advises.

CALL FOR HELP

While vomiting is usually caused by nothing more than a little indigestion, it's also a common symptom in dogs with serious stomach or intestinal problems, such as ulcers. The only time veterinarians really worry about vomiting is when dogs are doing it frequently, even when they haven't eaten, and when the vomit contains blood. In addition, vomiting that's accompanied by other symptoms, such as diarrhea or a fever, should be checked out by a veterinarian.

Give them ice cubes. Most dogs enjoy crunching ice, and it's a great way for them to take in essential fluids without getting too much all at once.

Give them a little salt. One way to calm an upset stomach is to give dogs a teaspoon of salt dissolved in eight ounces of warm water, says Bill Martin, D.V.M., a veterinarian in private practice in Fletcher, North Carolina. "The chloride ions in the salt calm the stomach," he says.

Or give them a soft drink. Another way to relieve nausea is to give dogs a small amount of a carbonated soft drink such as lemon-lime or ginger ale. The fizz seems to calm the stomach, and the sugar in the soft drink coats and soothes the stomach, says Dr. Carey. Give medium-size dogs about a table-spoon of the drink every 30 minutes, repeating

Crunching ice cubes gives a dog who's been sick a controlled ration of the fluid needed to make up for losses from dehydration, and satisfies a dog's urge to chew as well.

it three or four times. Very small dogs can have about a teaspoon at a time, and very big dogs can have two tablespoons, he adds.

FAST FIX A quick way to relieve stomach upsets is to give dogs Pepto-Bismol or Kaopectate, says Dr. Miller. She recommends giving one teaspoon of medicine for every 20 pounds of dog every six to eight hours. Most dogs detest the taste of these medicines, so you'll probably need to shoot it into their mouths with a plastic eye dropper or a turkey baster.

To do this, raise the muzzle so that it points slightly upward. Put the dropper or baster between the lips and the teeth, and slowly push a little bit of the medicine out. Wait until your dog swallows, then squeeze in a little more. Keep doing this until the entire dose is gone.

POOCH ?? PUZZLER

Why do dogs eat grass?

Dogs who are feeling off-color will often head straight for the first patch of green grass and begin munching away. Veterinarians still aren't sure if dogs eat grass because it helps them vomit whatever is causing them to feel bad, or if they get sick because the grass irritates their digestive systems.

There's no question that grass acts as an irritant in the stomach, says Dan Carey, D.V.M., a veterinarian with the Iams pet food company in Dayton, Ohio. But whether dogs actually think of grass as medicine or they simply like the taste, no one can say.

Weight Gain

Our dogs' ancestors lived at a time when food wasn't easy to come by, and starvation was always around the corner. They survived by the simple expedient of feasting whenever they were lucky enough to get a meal. By stuffing themselves, they were more likely to survive the lean times ahead.

Dogs don't have to worry about their next meal anymore, but they continue to think of food as something to gobble in a hurry—and the more food they get, the happier they are. Add to this the fact that humans get a lot of pleasure out of handing over treats and overfilling food bowls, and it's hardly surprising that there are so many pudgy pets out there.

The Usual Suspects

Overeating. The main cause of overweight, of course, is eating too much. Modern commercial foods are high in fat—not because dogs necessarily need all those extra calories, but because fat makes their food taste good. In addition, dogs often get a smorgasbord of snacks—a biscuit here, a tender piece of chicken there. The calories add up. "How about the person who goes to the refrigerator at one o'clock in the morning after watching the late show and makes himself a sandwich?" says Roger Caras, president of the American Society for the

> ## HEALTHFUL TREATS FOR DOGS
>
> Some commercial treats are high in calories, and it doesn't take many to ruin a dog's figure. You may prefer to try the following homestyle treats.
>
> • Bake fresh liver in a low oven until it's chewy, then cut it into little pieces. For extra appeal, sprinkle the liver with a little garlic powder before baking.
>
> • Cut hotdogs into tiny pieces and microwave them until they're crisp. For treats that are lower in fat, use turkey-based franks.
>
> • Carrots and other raw vegetables, such as green beans, are healthful, tasty canine snacks. If your dog won't eat them raw, steam or boil them in a little beef or chicken stock to add extra flavor.

Prevention of Cruelty to Animals. "The family dog is sure to follow him and say, 'What about me?' and get an extra meal as well."

Under-exercising. There's a very simple equation that determines whether dogs live lean or large: When the calories that they consume exceed the number of calories burned, the extra calories have to go somewhere—and that somewhere is usually in the padding next to the ribs, says Tim Banker, D.V.M., a veterinarian in private practice in Greensboro, North Carolina. For many dogs, the day's biggest calorie burn is when they walk to the food bowl. Owners don't always have the time or inclination for a lot of exercise either, which means their dogs get fewer walks and other forms of exercise.

Hormone imbalances. Dogs will occasionally gain weight when they produce too little thyroid hormone, the hormone that regulates the body's metabolism. As thyroid levels drop, dogs lose energy and start gaining weight. This condition, called hypothyroidism, can be quite serious. Once it's diagnosed, however, it's easy to treat by giving dogs thyroid supplements.

The Best Care

Start with a weight check. Dogs usually gain weight so slowly that the people in their lives don't notice anything's different—until they see the evidence on the veterinarian's scale. Some people weigh their pets every day—easy when you have a toy poodle, not so easy when you have a Great Dane. An easier way to check your dog's weight is to look at his figure. Every breed is different, but all dogs should have a distinct waist behind the rib cage. In addition, you should be able to feel your dog's ribs through a slight layer of padding.

Set regular mealtimes. It's convenient to feed dogs buffet-style by leaving food in the

Dogs who are at a healthy weight will have a distinct waist and a slight amount of padding on the ribs.

bowl for them to pick at. Some dogs show admirable restraint, but others insist on cleaning up—and then they ask for more. Rather than making food available all the time, veterinarians recommend establishing regular mealtimes once or twice a day.

Check the quantities. Even when people make the effort to watch calories, there's a tendency to give dogs too much food, says Jane Shaw, D.V.M., an instructor in the department of anatomy at the College of Veterinary Medicine at Cornell University in Ithaca, New York. When you pour out a bowlful, for example, do you use a measuring cup or do you pour "about a cup"? Dr. Shaw recommends measuring the food after you've poured it out. You may be amazed to learn how much you're actually giving.

Customize the diet. Every dog needs different amounts of food. The instructions on the bag provide a starting point, but you should ask

BREED SPECIFIC

Dogs with the highest risk of developing hypothyroidism—and the resulting weight gain—include Doberman pinschers, boxers, English bulldogs, dachshunds (right), Great Danes, and Old English sheepdogs.

CALL FOR HELP

Being overweight doesn't always mean that dogs are spending too much time at the trough. Some dogs develop a potbelly even when the rest of their bodies are thin. This may be caused by a condition called abdominal distension, in which fluids leak into the abdomen and cause the belly to swell. Abdominal distension may be caused by a viral infection, and it can be quite serious. If you suddenly notice a bulge where there wasn't one before, you'll want to call your vet right away.

your veterinarian for more specific directions. To help dogs slim down, you can cut back the amount you feed them by about 25 percent, says C. A. Tony Buffington, D.V.M., Ph.D., professor of veterinary clinical sciences at Ohio State University Veterinary Hospital in Columbus. If they haven't lost weight in two weeks, reduce the amount a bit more. If they still haven't lost weight, you'll need to ask your vet for help. A safe weight-loss limit is between 0.5 and 2 percent of a dog's weight each week, Dr. Buffington adds. If you have a 100-pound dog, for example, he can safely lose about 1 pound a week.

Feed them more often. The problem with diets is the constant feeling of hunger. To keep dogs feeling satisfied, Dr. Shaw recommends feeding them less food a little bit more often. Their total daily calories will be about the same, but the more frequent meals will help keep them comfortable.

Stick to healthy snacks. Your pet won't lose weight if he eats between meals. Try giving fewer between-meal snacks, or switch over to healthier snacks, such as raw vegetable sticks or popcorn cakes, says Dr. Shaw.

Be prepared for backsliding. Most dogs don't take kindly to changes in their culinary routines. They'll often resort to surreptitious kitchen raids—digging through the trash or nabbing food off the counter. Some dogs even learn to open the refrigerator, says Dr. Shaw. "In some cases, you can hardly live with an animal on a diet," she adds. "Hang in there. After a while, your pet will adjust."

Burn more calories. While cutting calories is an essential part of any weight-loss plan, you need to burn them as well. This is easy to do because most dogs love activities that get them moving—going for walks, chasing balls, or running around the yard, says Dr. Banker.

Dogs don't like dieting any more than people do. Dogs who need to lose weight should be watched in case they start backsliding.

Weight Loss

The combination of easy living and an abundance of food means that dogs gain weight almost as easily as people do. It's a lot less common, however, for them to lose weight. Except for dogs on diets, weight loss is nearly always a sign that a dog is ill, says Lynn Harpold, D.V.M., a veterinarian in private practice in Mesa, Arizona.

The Usual Suspects

Dental problems. Veterinarians have found that more than 85 percent of dogs over the age of three have some degree of periodontal disease, a condition in which bacteria and a variety of irritating substances work their way beneath the gums, causing painful infections or irritation. Periodontal disease that isn't treated can

CALL FOR HELP

Since weight loss may accompany dozens of internal illnesses, ranging from parasites to cancer, you'll want to call your veterinarian as soon as you notice that your dog is looking thinner than he used to be. Even though the problem may turn out to be a simple one, some of the conditions that cause dogs to lose weight will get worse very quickly unless they're treated, says Kenneth Lyon, D.V.M. a a veterinary dental specialist in private practice in Mesa, Arizona.

make eating very painful, and many dogs will simply quit, says Kenneth Lyon, D.V.M., a veterinary dental specialist in private practice in Mesa, Arizona. Other dental problems, such as a fractured tooth or an abscess, may also cause dogs to quit eating, he adds.

Competition. Even easygoing dogs can get very aggressive about food. In families with a number of dogs, it's not uncommon for one dog to be both greedy and assertive and to steal his companions' suppers. Most dogs will protect their food, but some are so timid about confrontations that they'll simply walk away. Eventually, of course, they may start losing weight.

Pain. Dogs lose their appetites when they're not feeling well. This is especially common in older dogs who may have arthritis or problems with their hips or other joints. The discomfort takes away their appetites, and even when they're hungry, they may have difficulty getting up and walking to the food bowl.

Stress. The fast pace of modern life can be very stressful for dogs, who don't respond to changes very well. Dogs who are anxious or nervous—because their owners are away from home more than usual, for example—may stop eating, says Dr. Harpold. This type of weight loss is rarely serious, however, because they'll start eating properly again once things calm down.

High-energy living. Modern dog foods contain an abundance of nutrients, and most dogs get all the calories they need. Dogs who burn a lot of calories, however, such as working dogs or those who have given birth, may lose weight because they're getting fewer calories than they need, says Kevin O'Neall, D.V.M., a veterinarian in private practice in Green River, Wyoming. Eating plans for these problems need to be custom-designed. Your veterinarian will advise you on a plan that's best for your dog.

Diabetes. The hormone insulin is responsible for transporting the sugars in foods into the body's cells. Dogs with diabetes don't have enough insulin, which means that no matter how much they eat, they aren't getting all the calories they need.

The Best Care

Take care of their teeth. The ideal way to keep the teeth and gums healthy is to brush them once or twice a week, either by using a brush and a pet toothpaste or by rubbing the surfaces of the teeth with a piece of gauze, says Ehud Sela, D.V.M., a veterinarian in private practice near Fort Lauderdale, Florida. Moistening the gauze with chicken or beef broth will encourage your dog to hold still for the cleaning, he adds.

An easier way to keep the teeth healthy is to feed your dog dry food. Unlike wet foods, which stick to the teeth, dry foods are slightly abrasive, so they help scour the teeth with every meal. In addition, you can buy canine dental toys at pet supply stores. These toys have nubs or ridges that help scrape deposits off the teeth every time your dog chomps down.

Feed dogs separately. For some dogs, the instinct to steal food is a lot stronger than their desire to play by the rules. About all you can do to reduce mealtime competition is to feed dogs

Older dogs with arthritis may be reluctant to get up to walk to their food bowls. Putting the bowls closer to their beds will make life easier for them.

separately, says Dr. Harpold. Once your dog is able to eat his supper in peace, he should start gaining weight within a few weeks.

Control the blood sugar. Veterinarians have found that dogs with diabetes generally do better when they're given several small meals a day instead of one big one. Your vet may also recommend giving your dog foods that are higher in fiber than standard grocery-store brands. High-fiber foods regulate and smoothe out the absorption of sugars into the bloodstream, making a sudden sugar low much less likely to occur.

Bring the food to them. Nothing is sadder than watching a dog try, without success, to lumber to his feet at suppertime. There isn't a cure for conditions such as arthritis, but you can make your dog's life easier by putting his food closer to where he sleeps. In addition, veterinarians sometimes recommend using an elevated food bowl so dogs don't have the added stress of bending their necks.

Credits and Acknowledgments

(t=top, b=bottom, l=left, r=right, c=center, F=front, C=cover, B=back).
All photographs are copyright to the sources listed below.

PHOTOGRAPH CREDITS

Ad-Libitum: Stuart Bowey vib, viit, viib, 14b, 18b, 18t, 21b, 22b, 24b, 26b, 28b, 30b, 34b, 36b, 37b, 38b, 39b, 44b, 47t, 48b, 52b, 53t, 54b, 57t, 58b, 60b, 61b, 62b, 65b, 67b, 68b, 69b, 71b, 72b, 73b, 75c, 76b, 77t, 78t, 80t, 82t, 85b, 85b, 87b, 88b, 89b, 91b, 92b, 98b, 99t, 101t, 104t, 107b, 111b, 112t, 113b, 115b, 116b, 117t, 119t, 122b, 123b, 126b, 128c, 134b, 137b, 138b, 138t, 139b, 140b, 141b, 141t, 143t, 144b, 146b, 146t, 152t, 153b, 156t, 158b, 158t, 159b, BClc, BCbl.

Animal Photography: Sally Anne Thompson 43b.

Auscape International: Gissey-COGIS, 56b; Hemmeline/Cogis, 161t; Jean-Michel Labat, 130b; Lanceau/Cogis, 114t; Yves Lanceau, 54t, 109t, 121t.

Bill Bachman and Associates: Bill Bachman, 13t, 79t.

Norvia Behling: viiib, 3b, 29t, 41t, 55t, 84t, 145b, 149b.

Bruce Coleman Limited: Adriano Bacchella, 118b, BCtr; Jane Burton, 46b, 93b, 143b, 154b, BCrc; Hans Reinhard, 20t.

Renee Lynn, Davis Lynn Images: FC

Matt Gavin-Wear: 125b.

Ron Kimball Photography: Ron Kimball, x.

NHPA: Henry Ausloos, 153t; Yves Lanceau, 74b.

Rodale Images: 95b; John P. Hamel, 16c.

Dale C. Spartas: 5c, 9b.

Judith E. Strom: 8b, 91t, 97b, 103t, BCtl.

ILLUSTRATIONS

Virginia Gray, 110br; **Chris Wilson/Merilake,** 25b, 32bc, 32bl, 33t, 45b, 59b, 72t, 84b, 129t, 133b.

The publisher would like to thank the following people for their assistance in the preparation of this book:
Maxine Fernandez; Tracey Jackson; Dr. Kenneth Lyon; Dr. Paul McGreevy; Dr. Bill Martin; Pets International; Denise Rainey; The Royal Society for the Prevention of Cruelty to Animals, Yagoona, N.S.W., Australia.
Special thanks to the following people who kindly brought their dogs to photo shoots:
Len Antcliff and "Bozie"; Leigh Audette and "Boss"; Felicity Bateman and "Bonnie"; Esther Blank and "Max"; Sally Blaxland and "Poppy"; Don Craig and "Sandy"; Julia Edworthy and "Bingo" and "Lucy"; Chloe Flutter and "Bob"; Matt Gavin-Wear and "Amber"; Kathy Gorman and "Carlo"; Robyn Hayes and "Patsy"; Dinah Holden and "Molly"; Anne Holmes and "Marli"; Suzie Kennedy and "Eddie"; Natalie Kidd and "Cisco"; Michael Lenton and "Jasper"; Bernadette McCaig and "Samson"; Paul McGreevy and "Wally"; Hilary Mulquin and "Cleo"; Dan Penny and "Jaffa" and "Molly"; Angela Price and "Bramble"; Moyna Smeaton and "Tilly"; Andrea Webster and "Max".

Index